TOH

THE TRY ON HAUL MAGAZINE

Try On Haul :

"A young and pretty girl that shows in social media clothing she buys, she gets as a gift or she tries as a model, as an influencer or as a new rising star"

Is with love for the art of photography that I make this magazine and photobook to show you my photo sessions with models and influencers from all over the world... ***Try on Haul*** *Style*

I hope you enjoy the images and much as I enjoyed doing them.

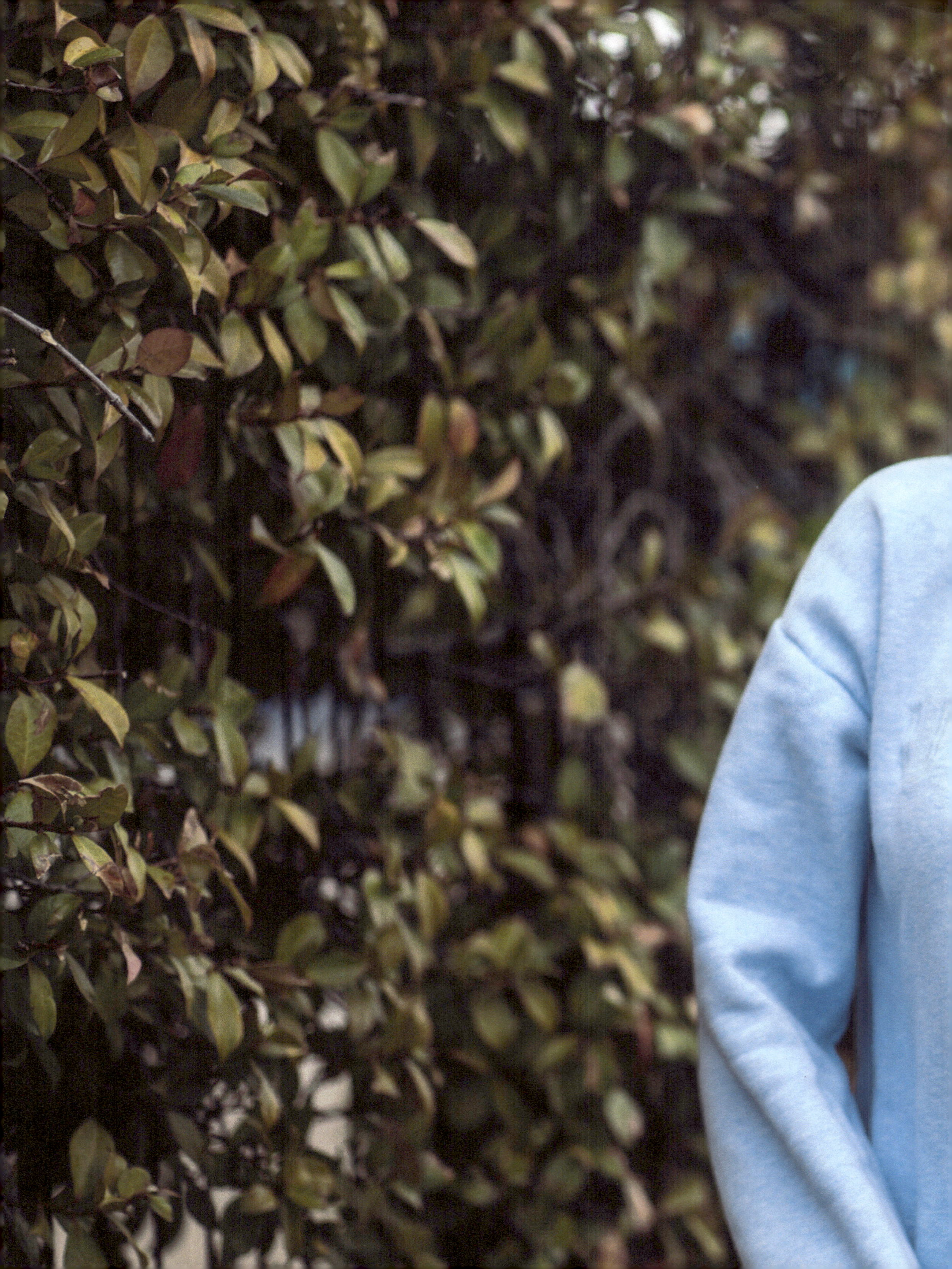

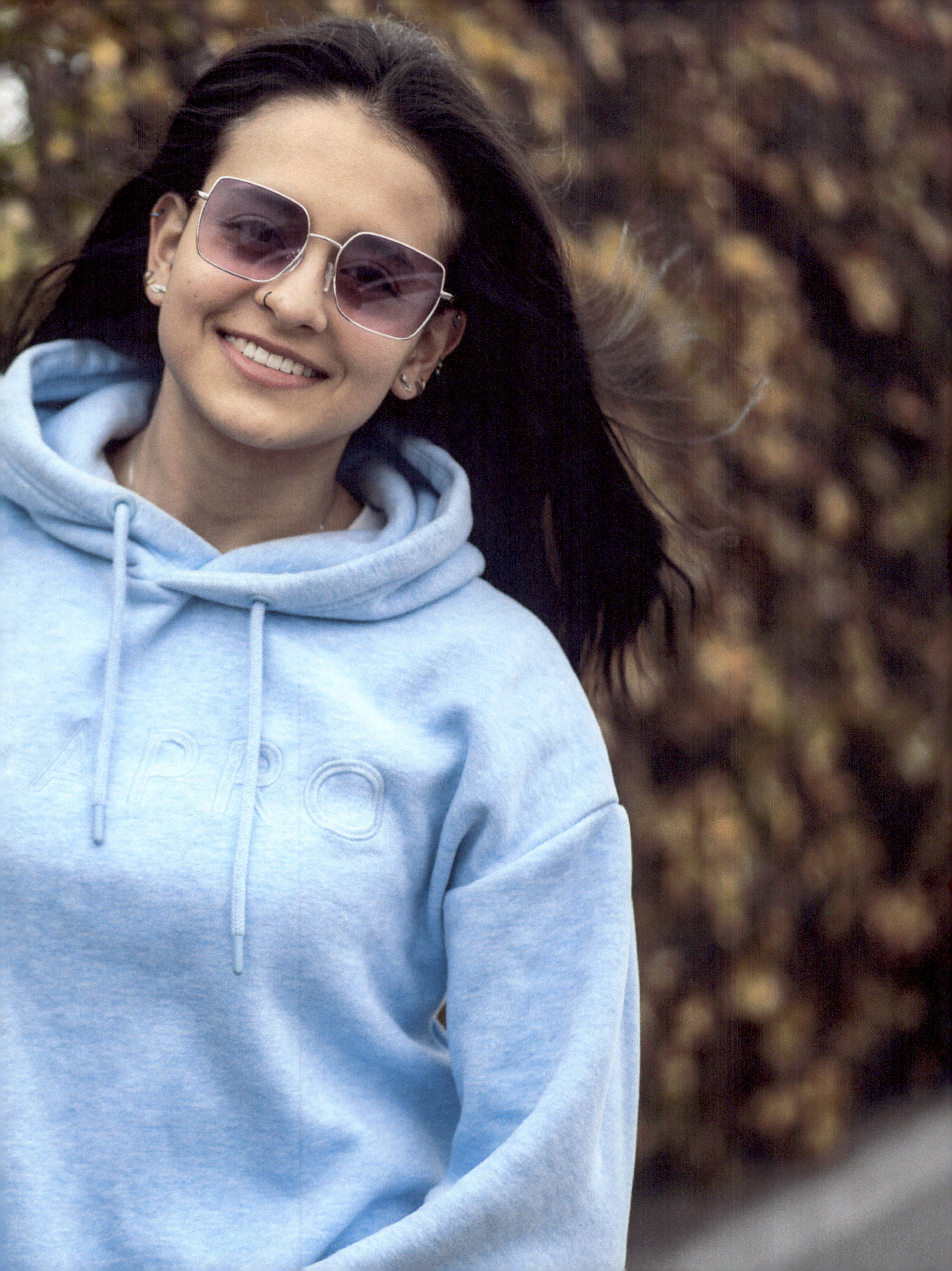
APRO

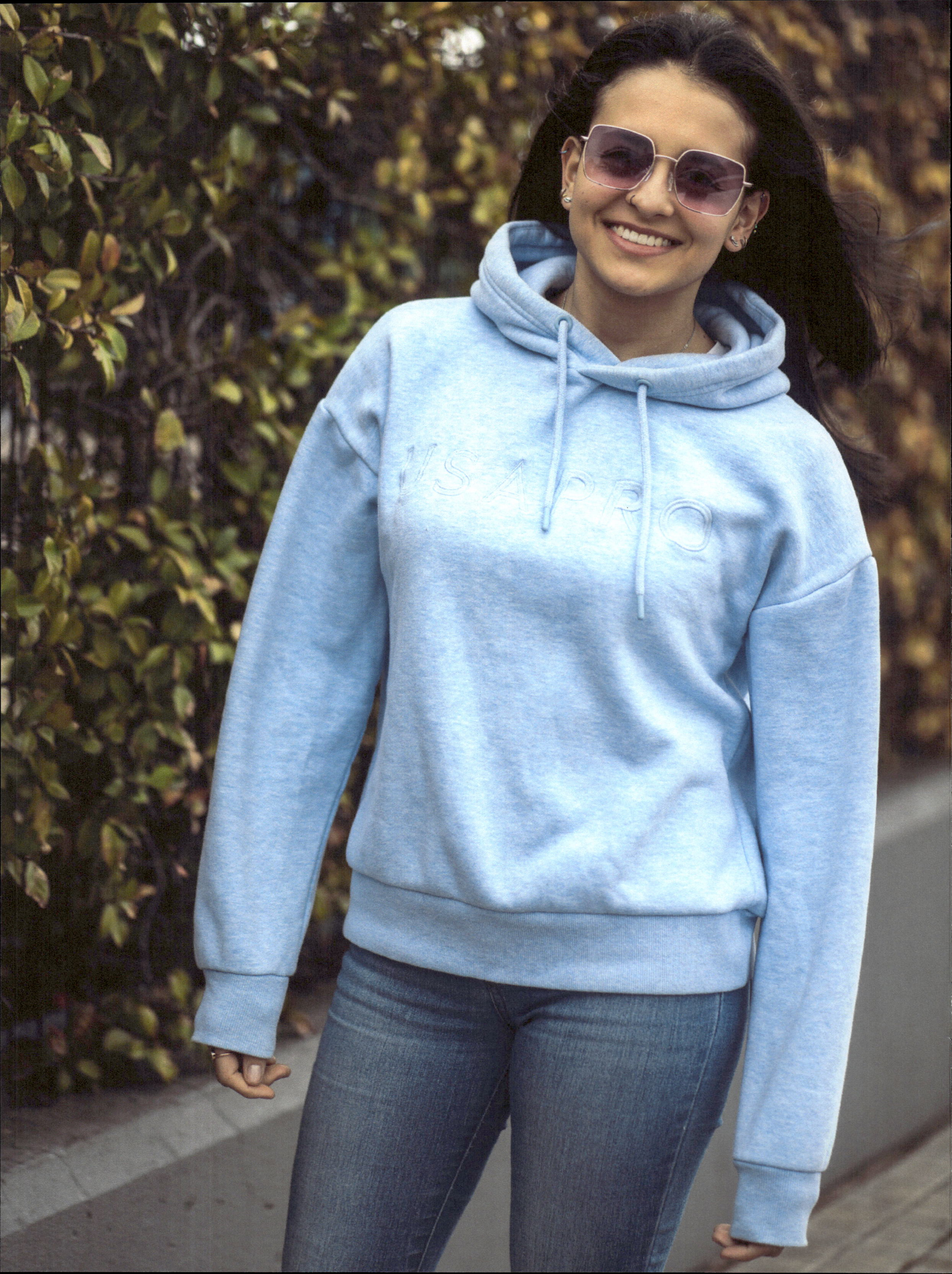
USAPRO

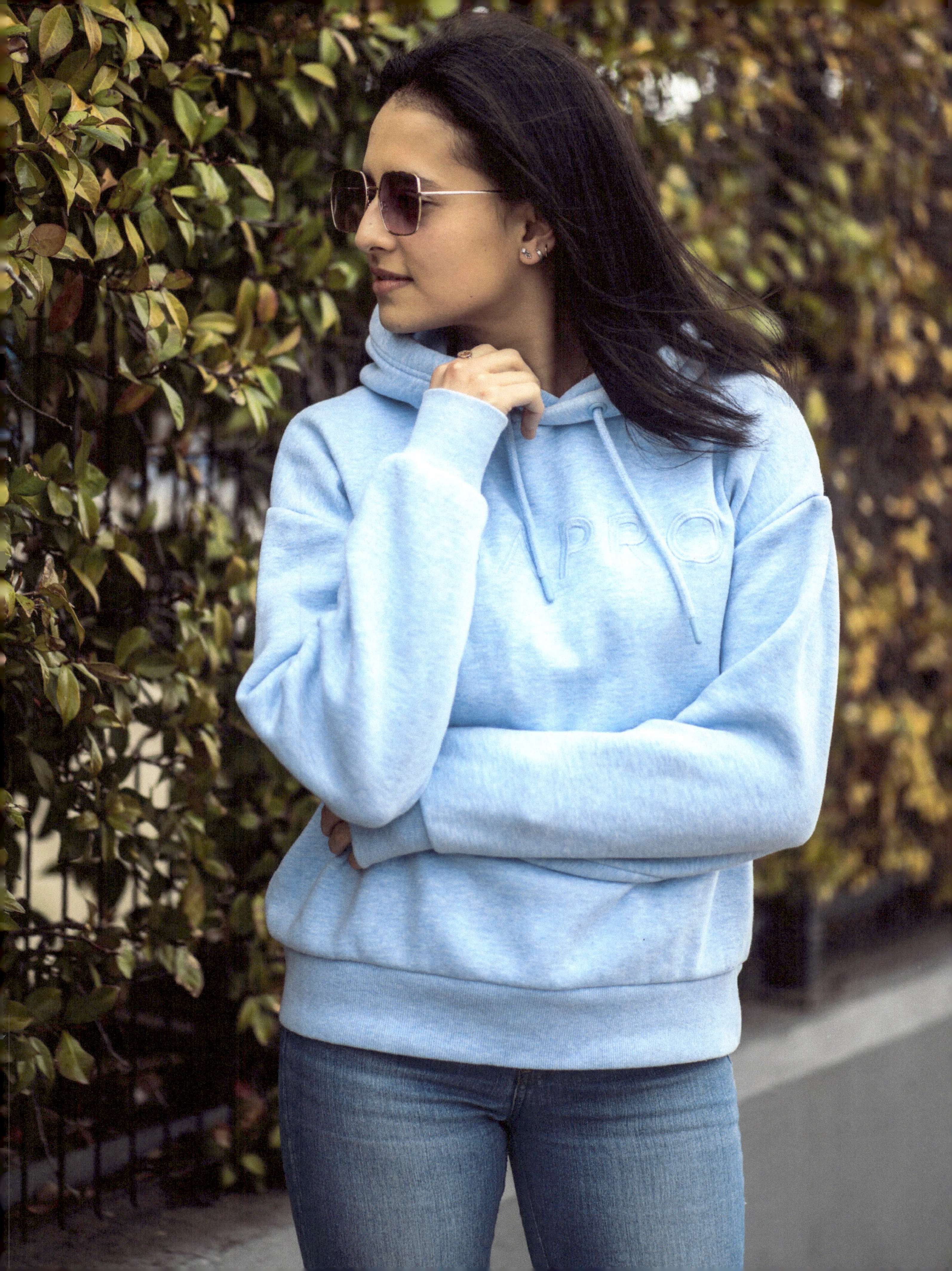

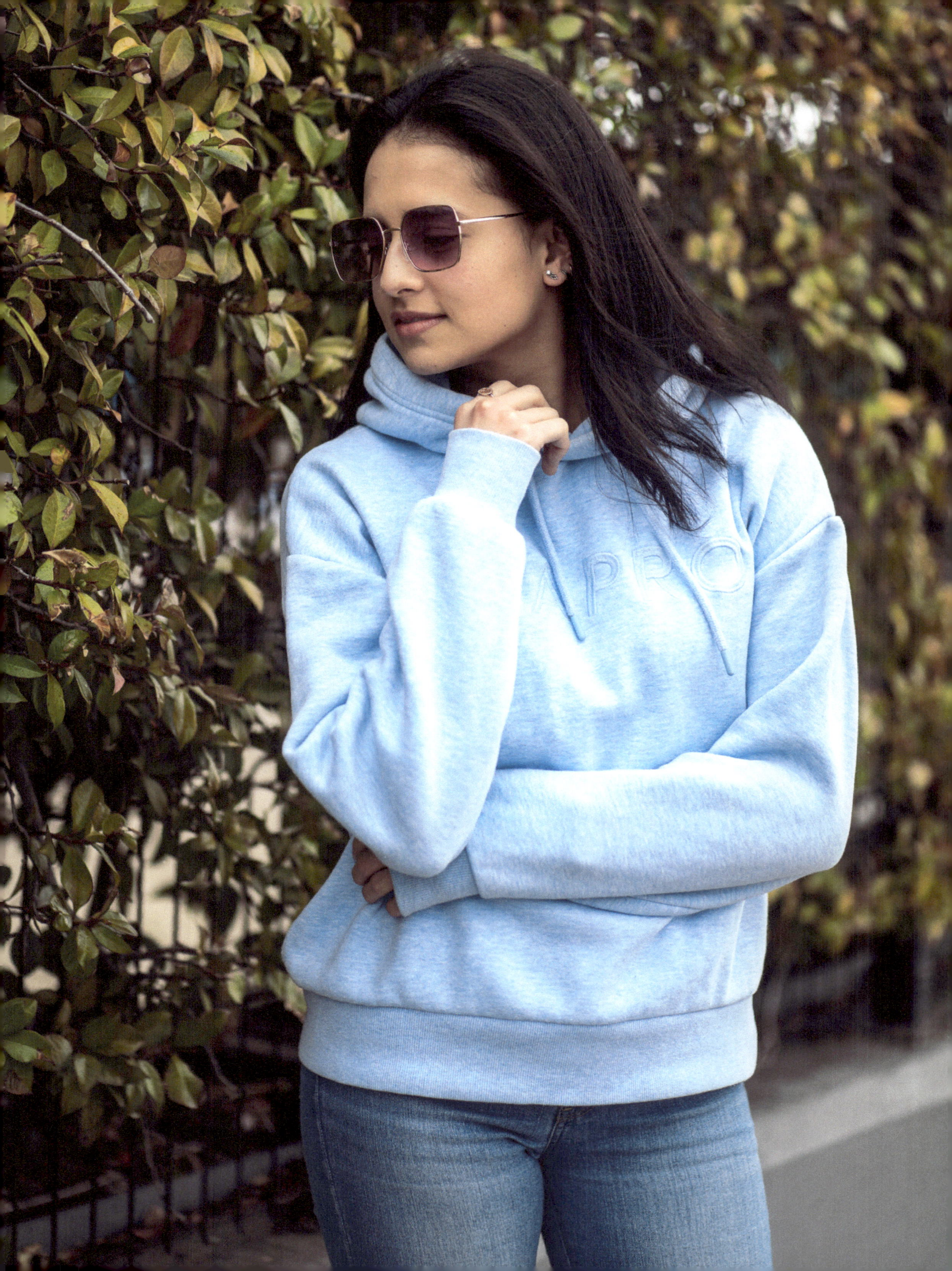

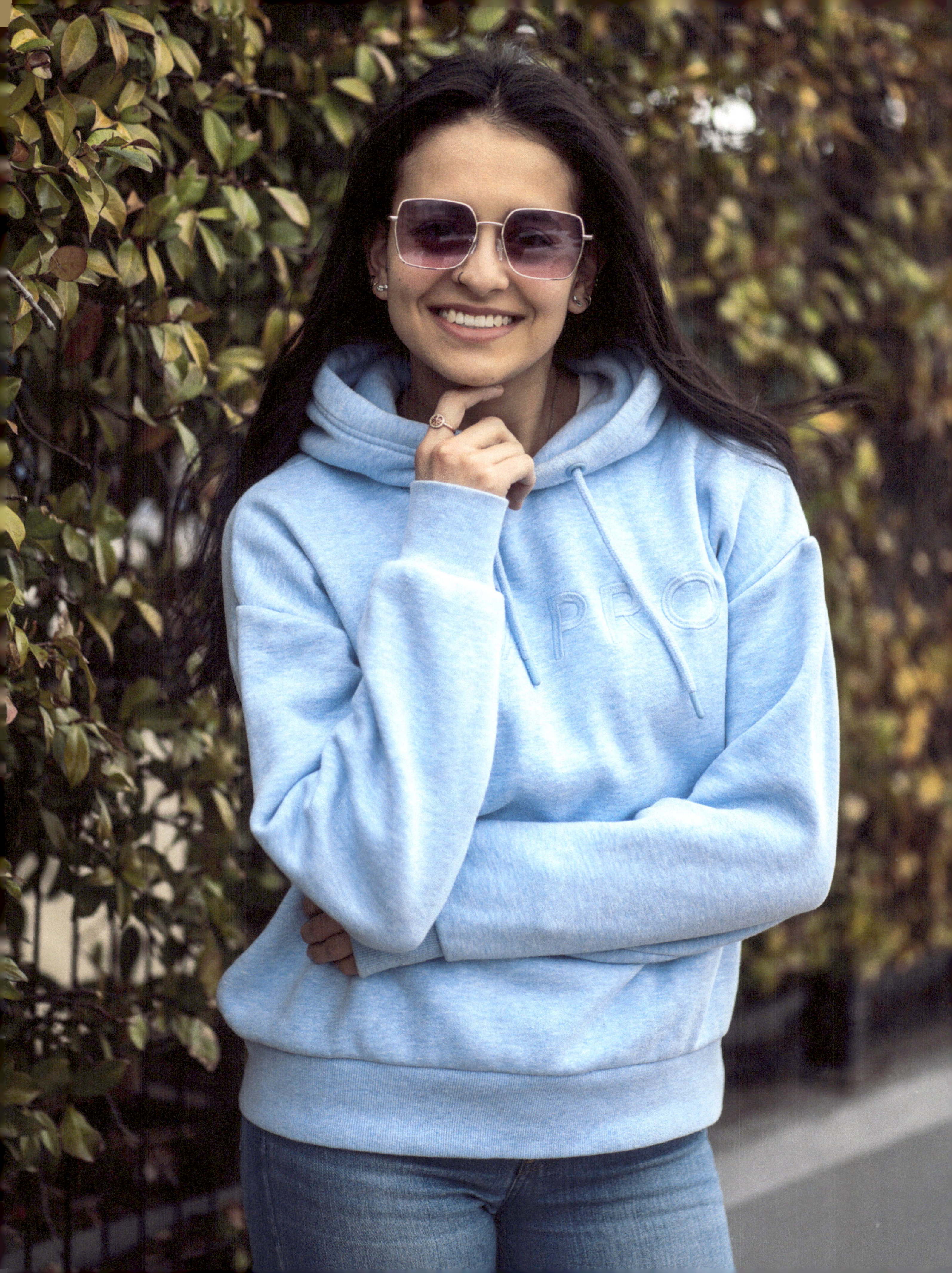

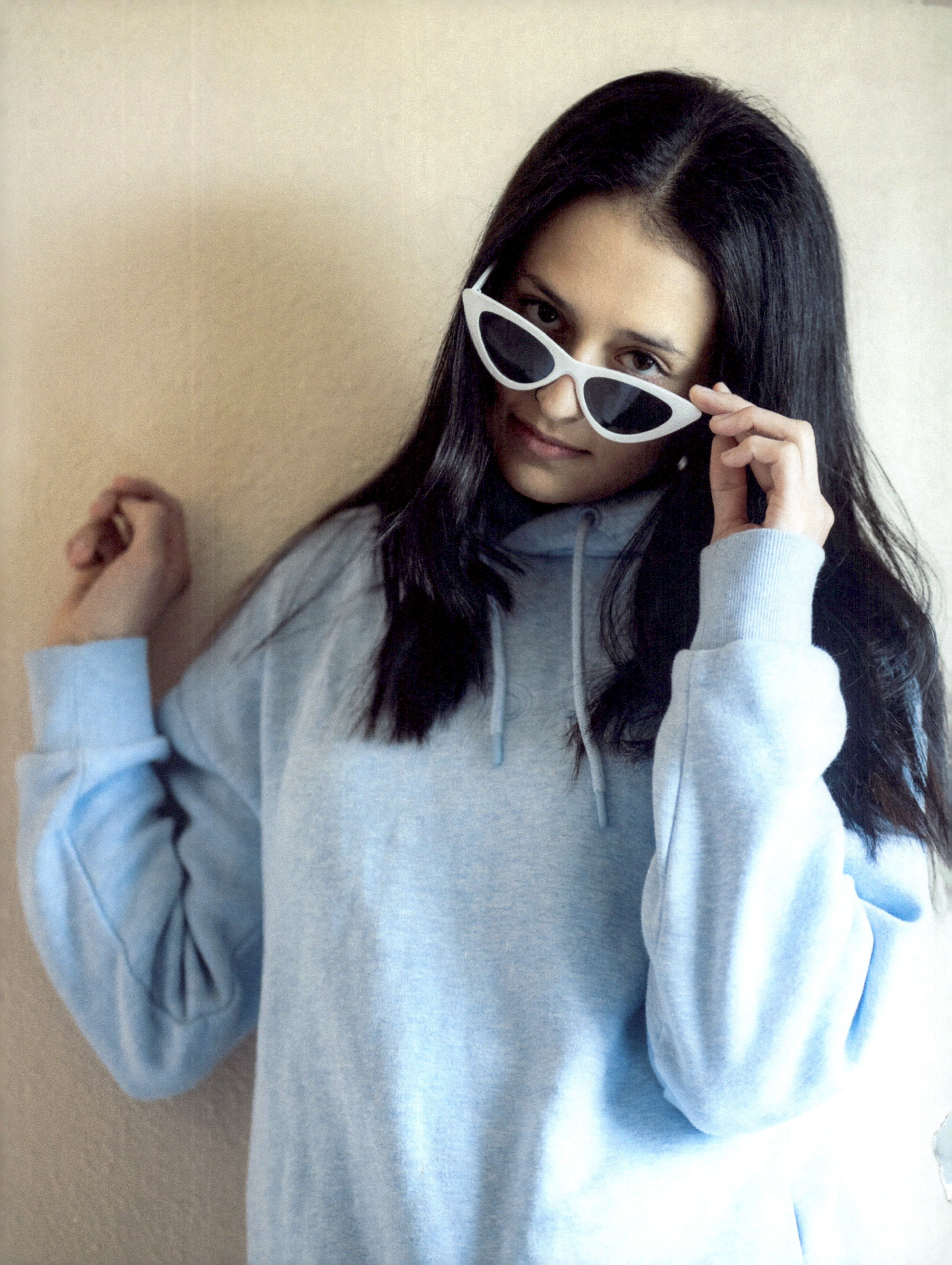

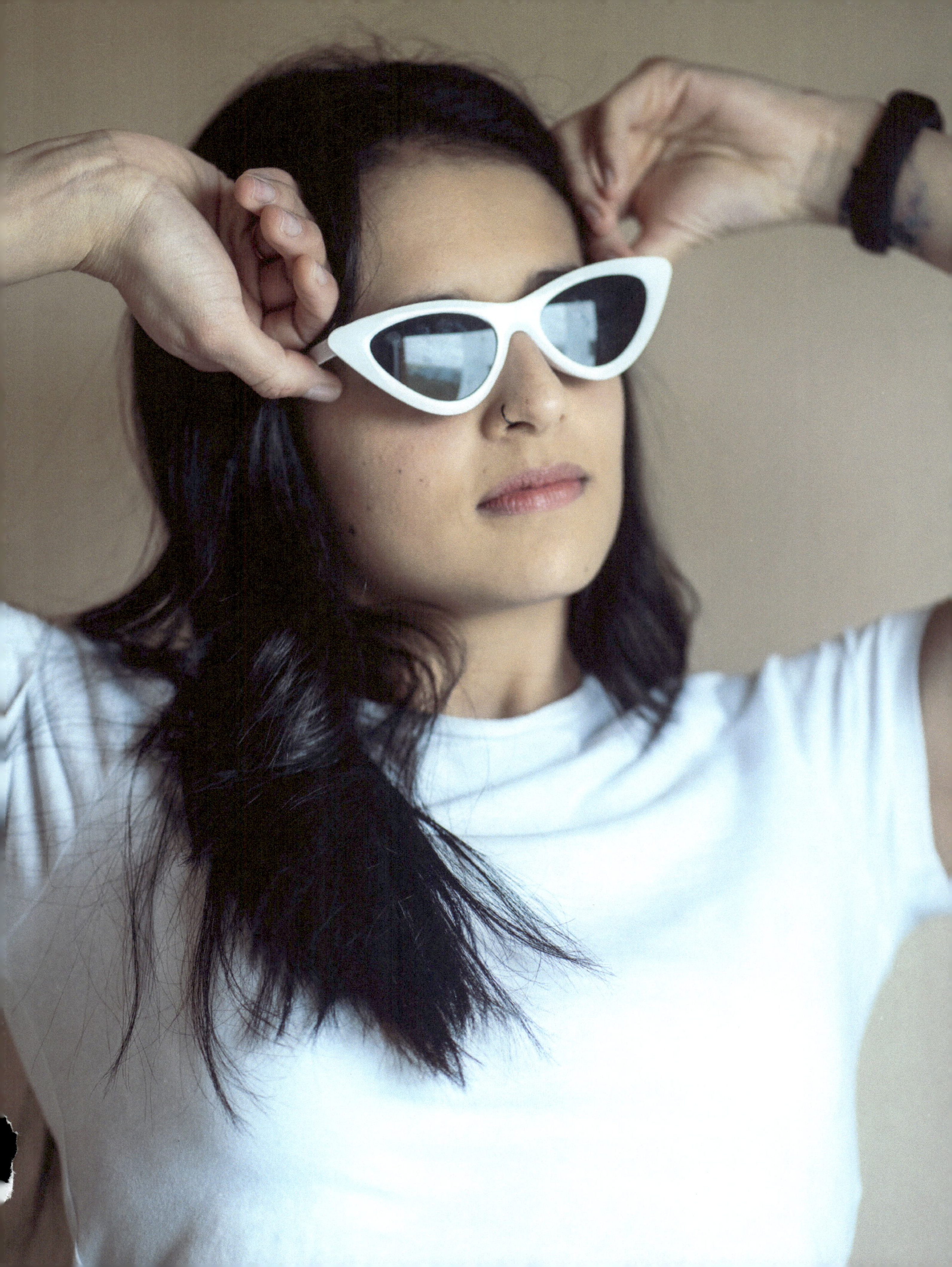

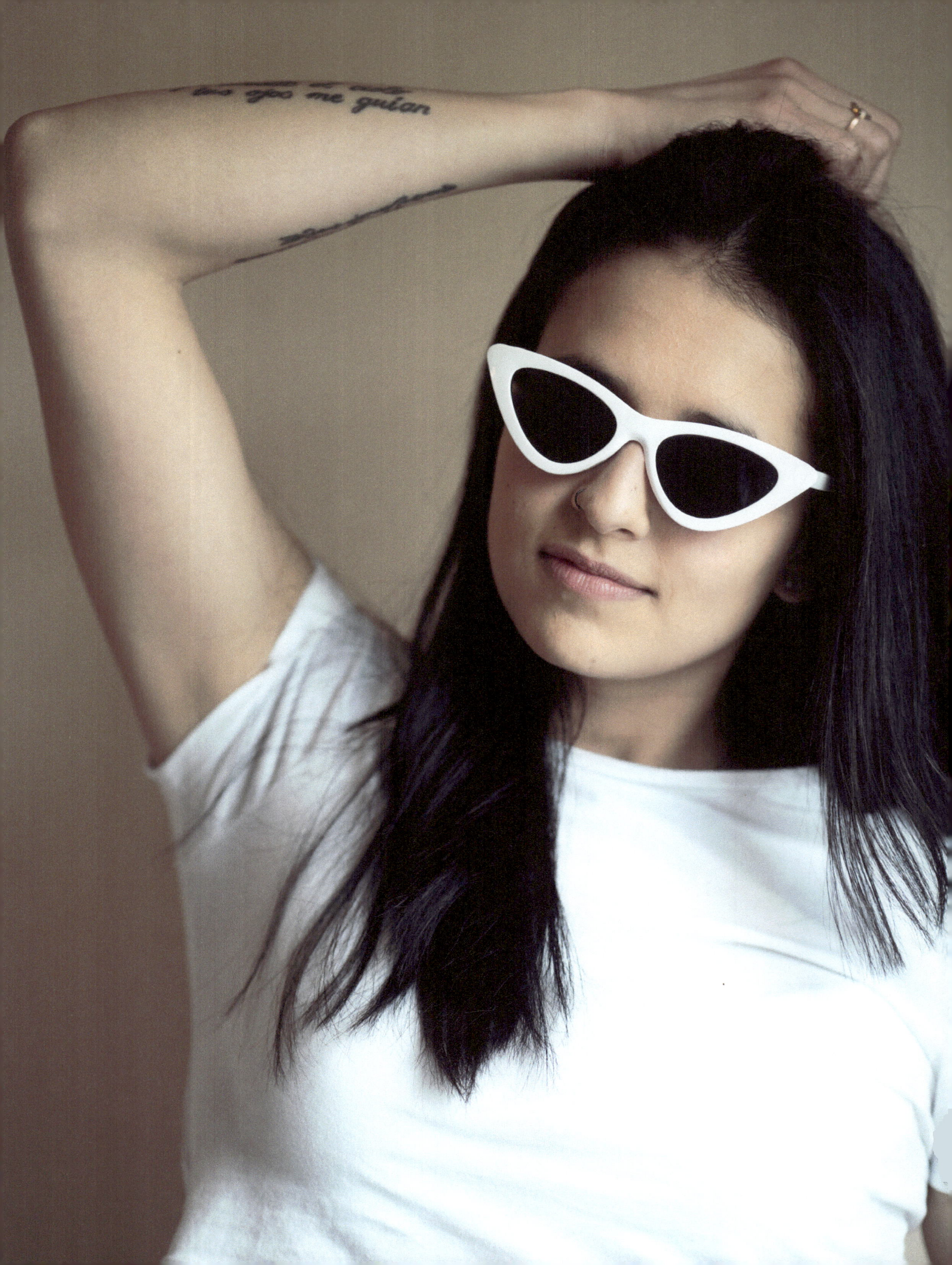

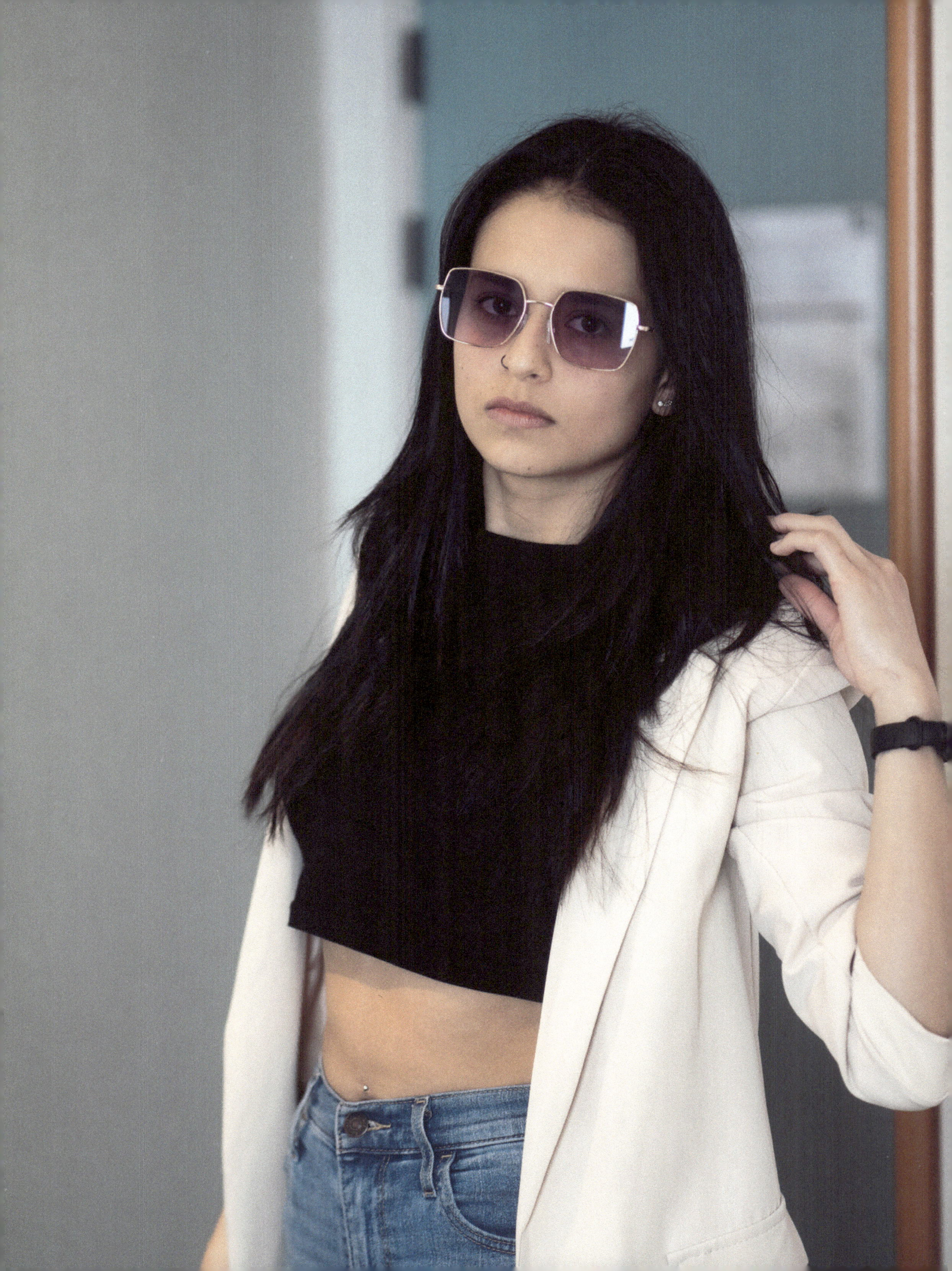

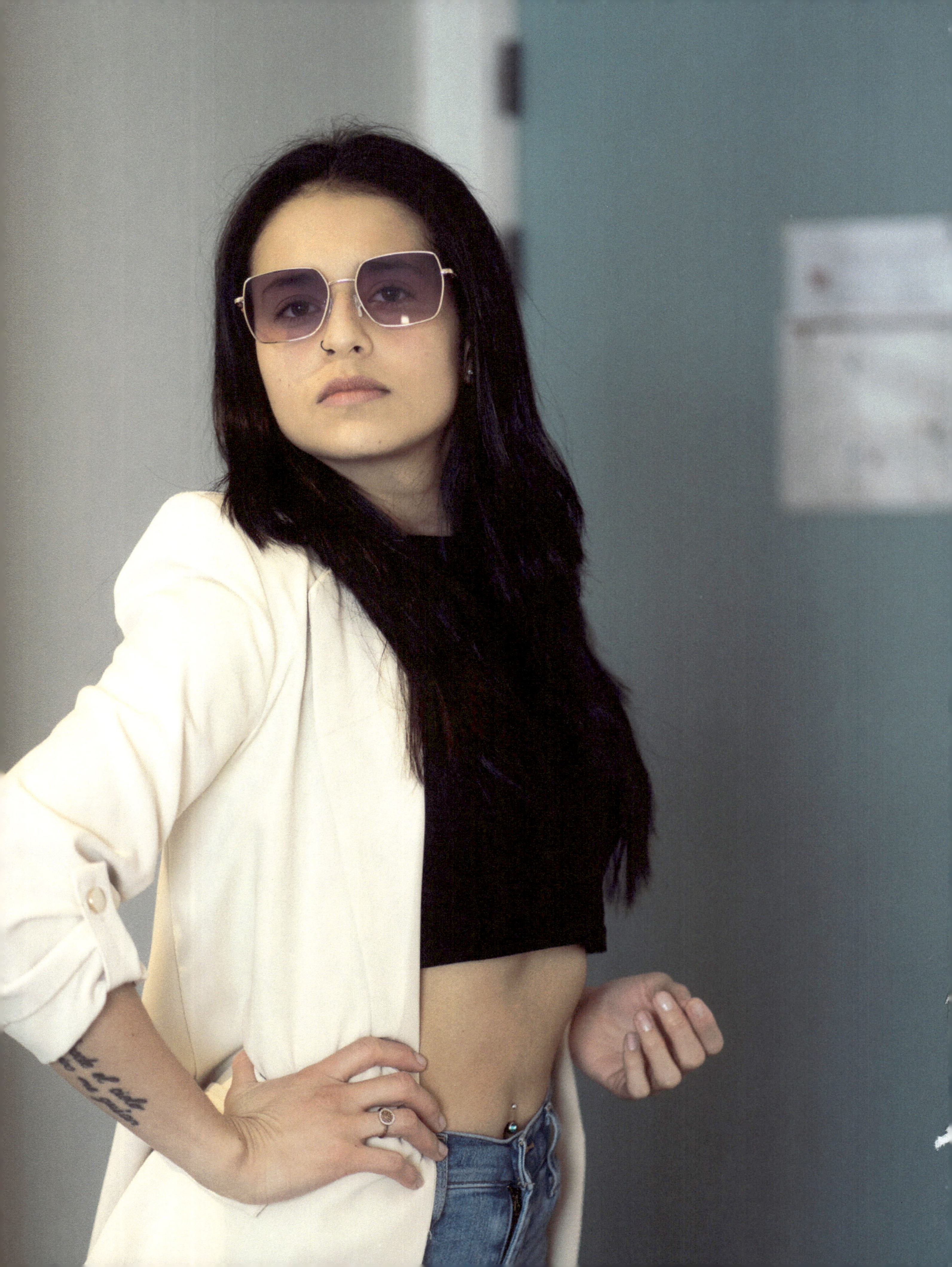

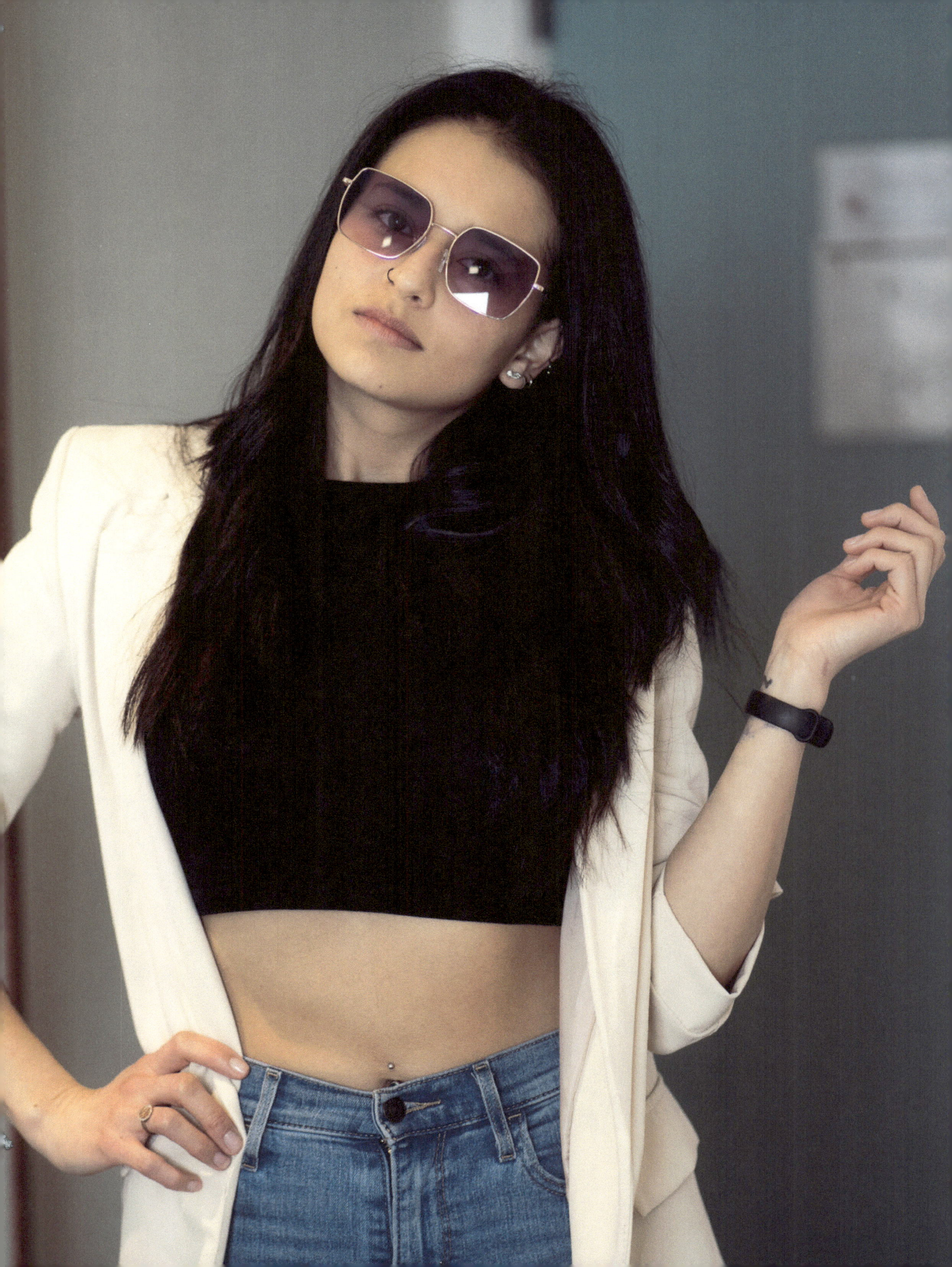

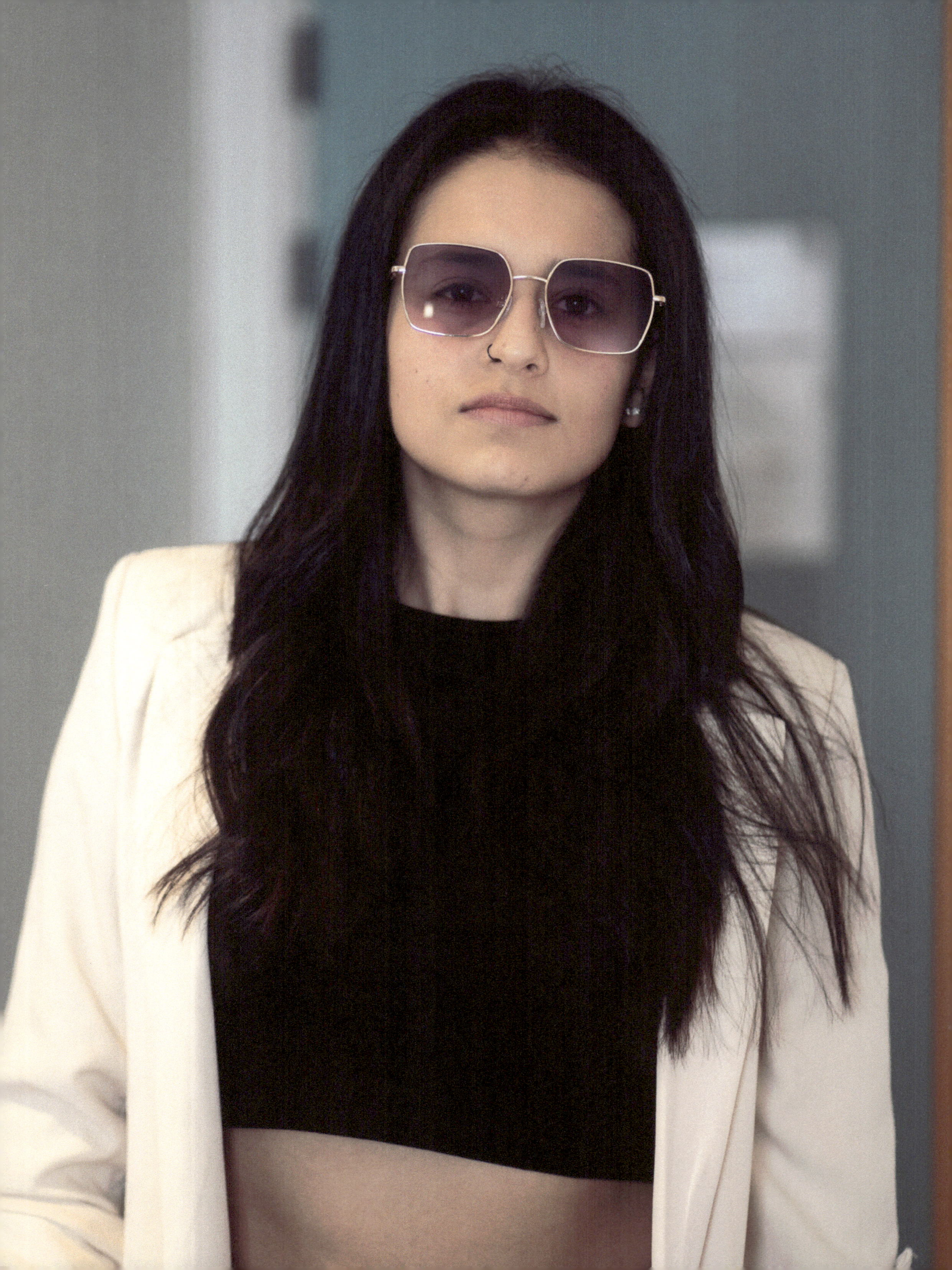

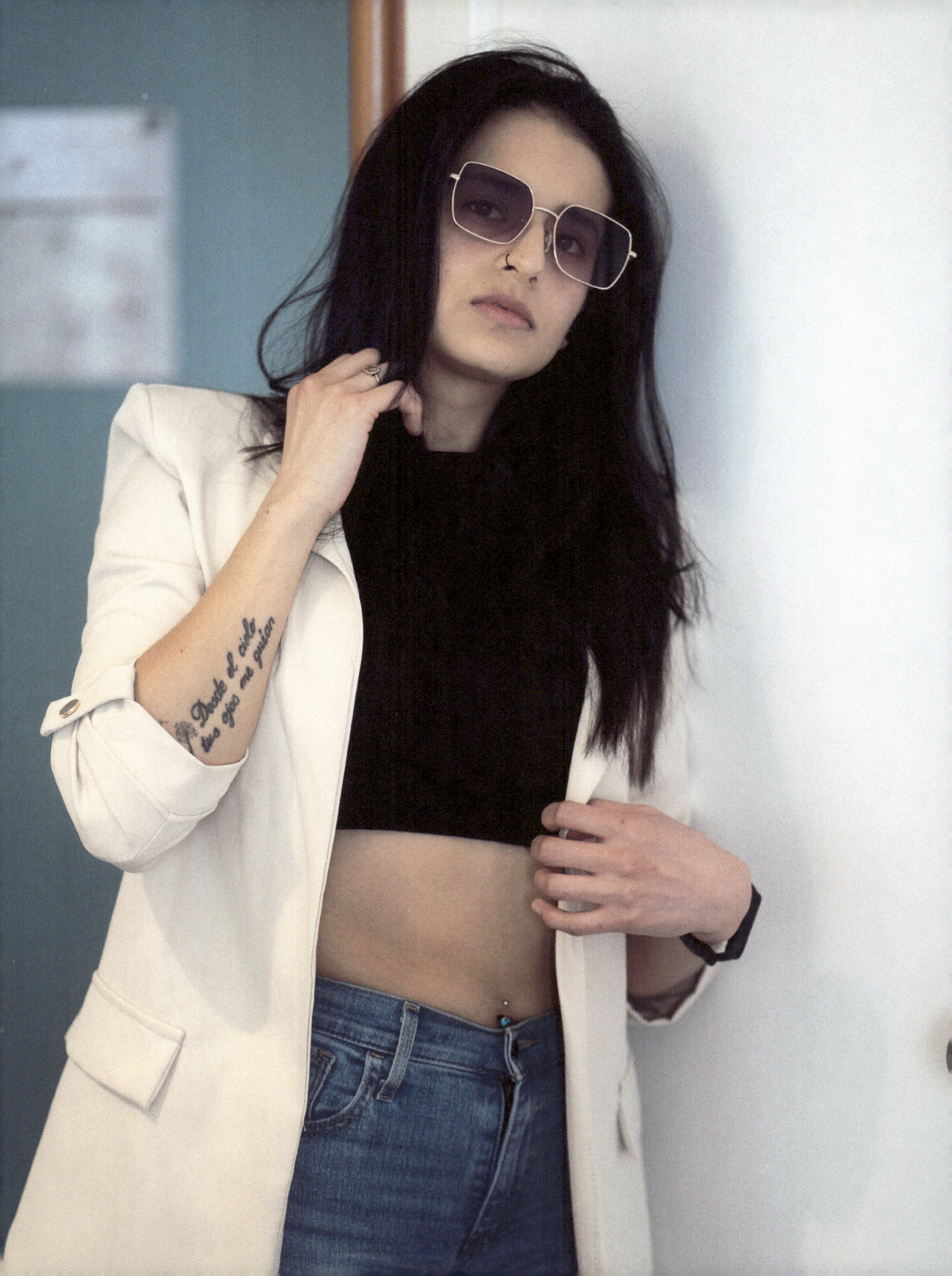
Desde el cielo
tus ojos me guian

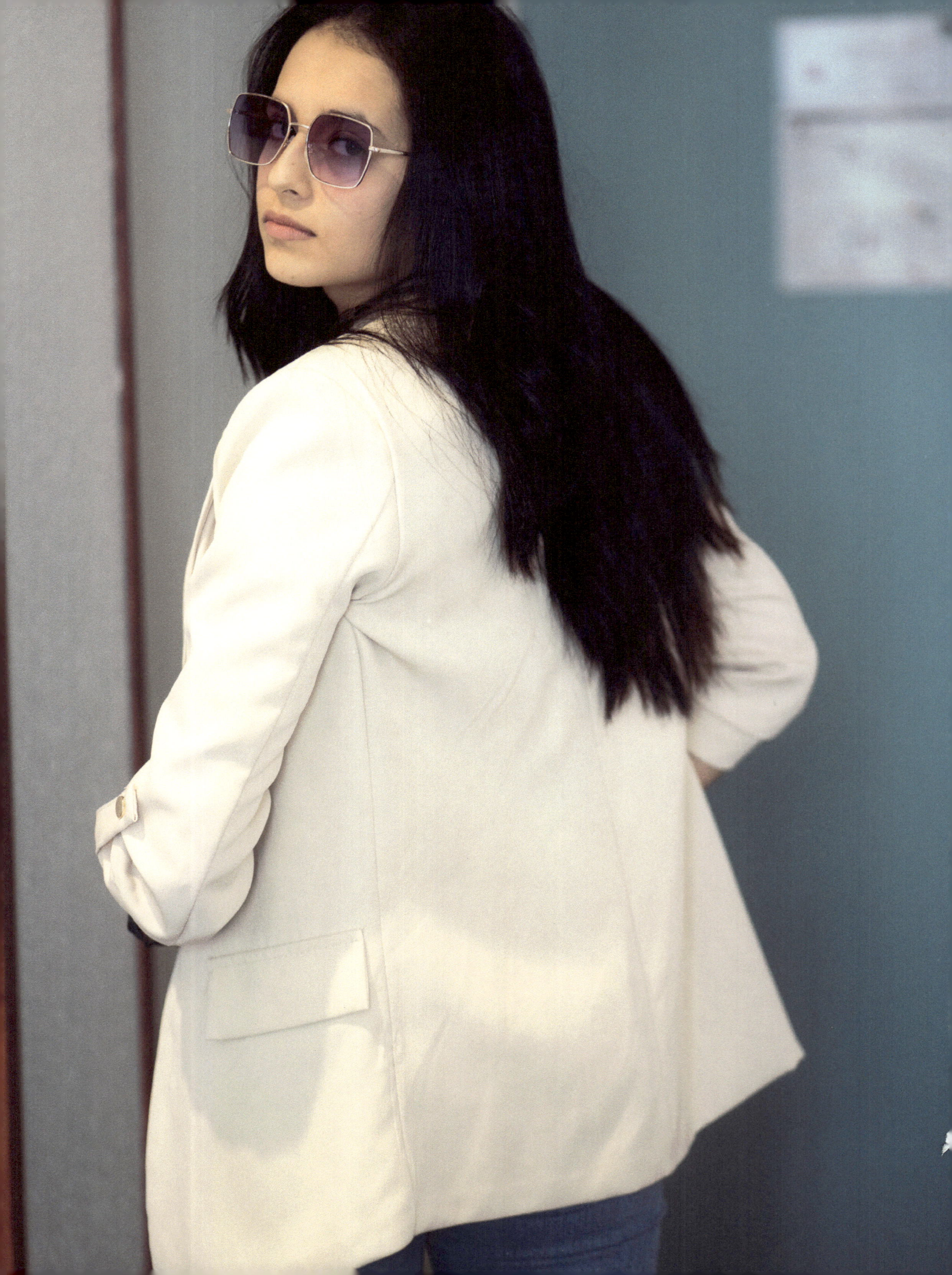

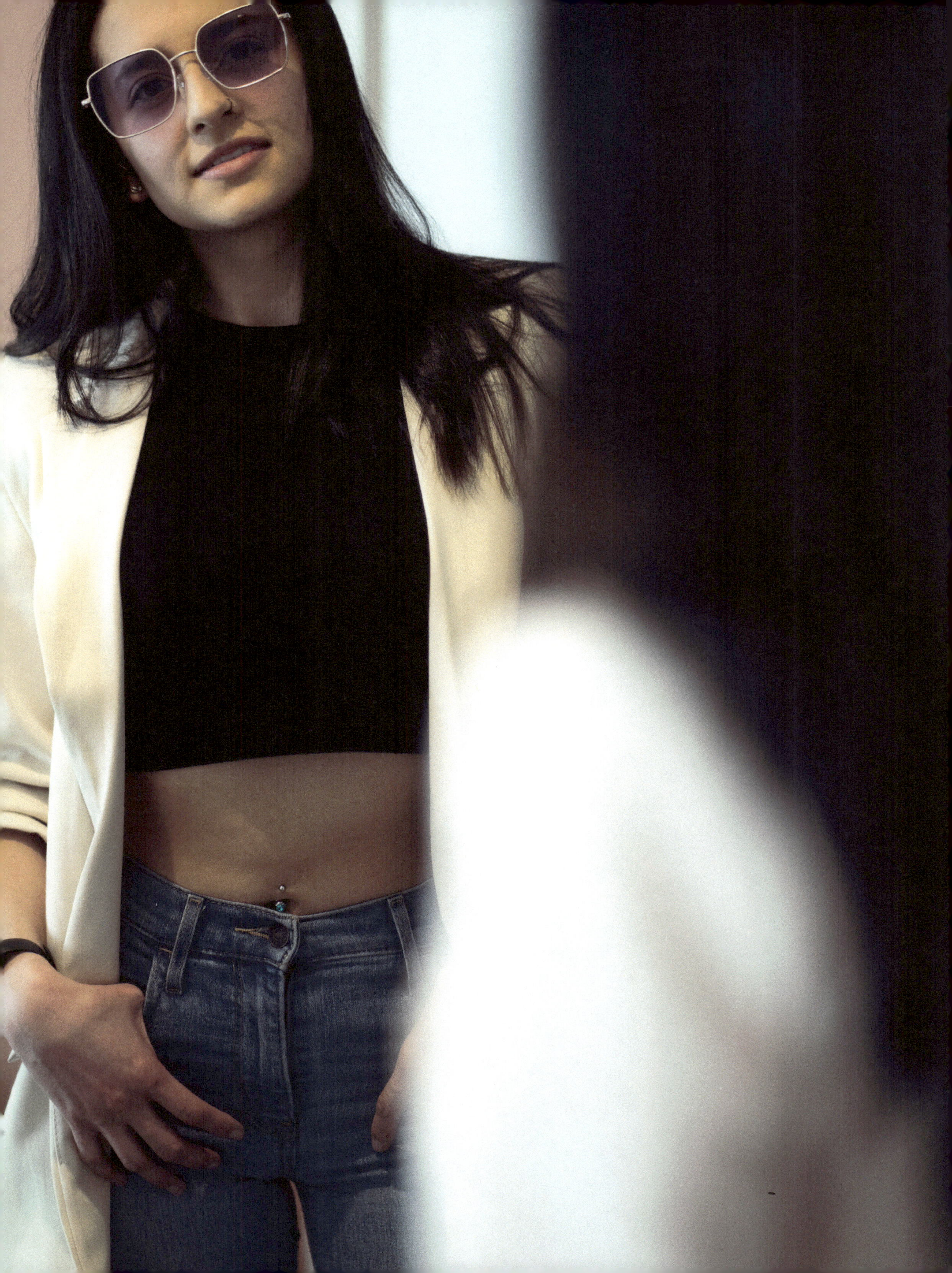

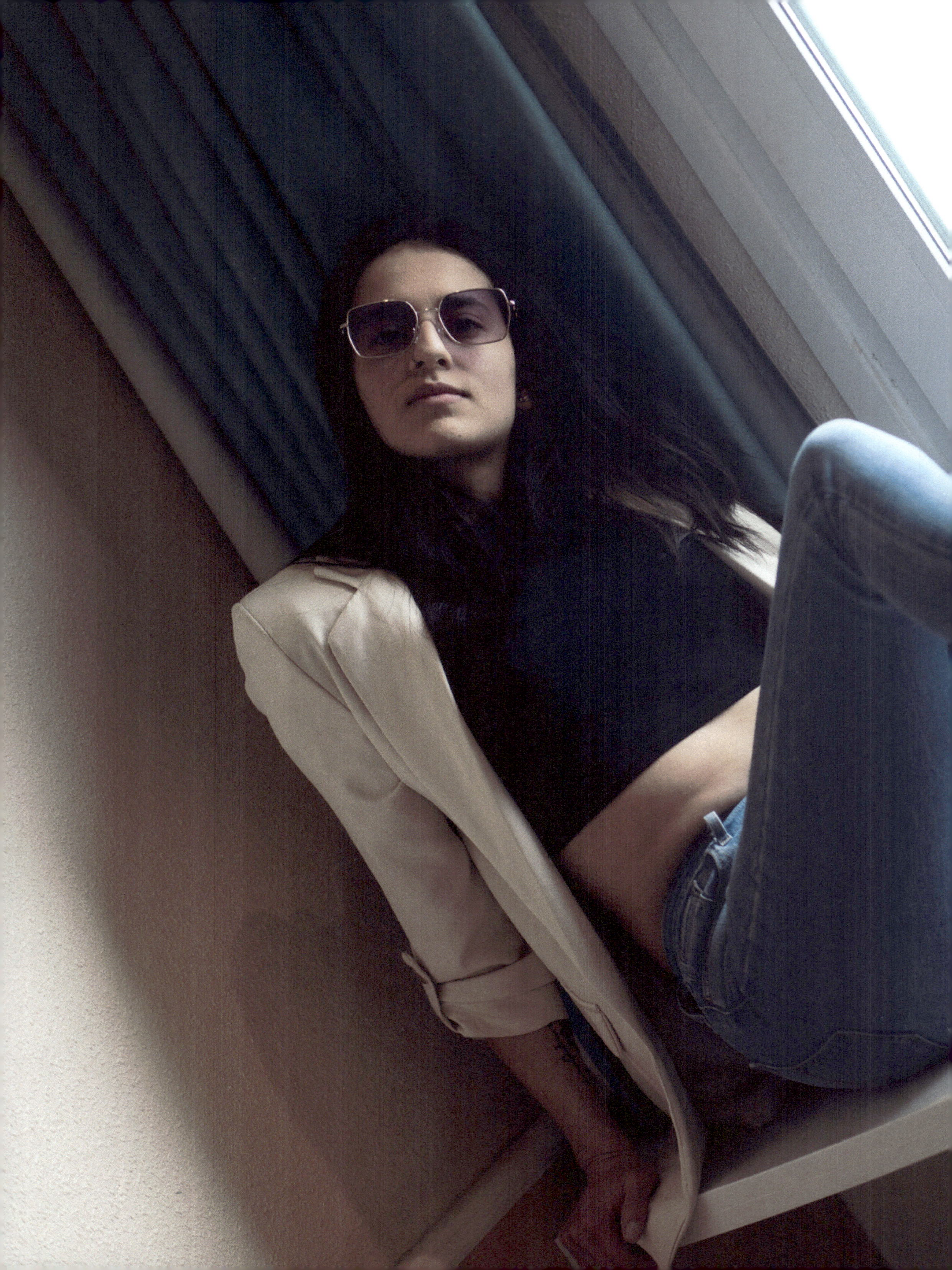

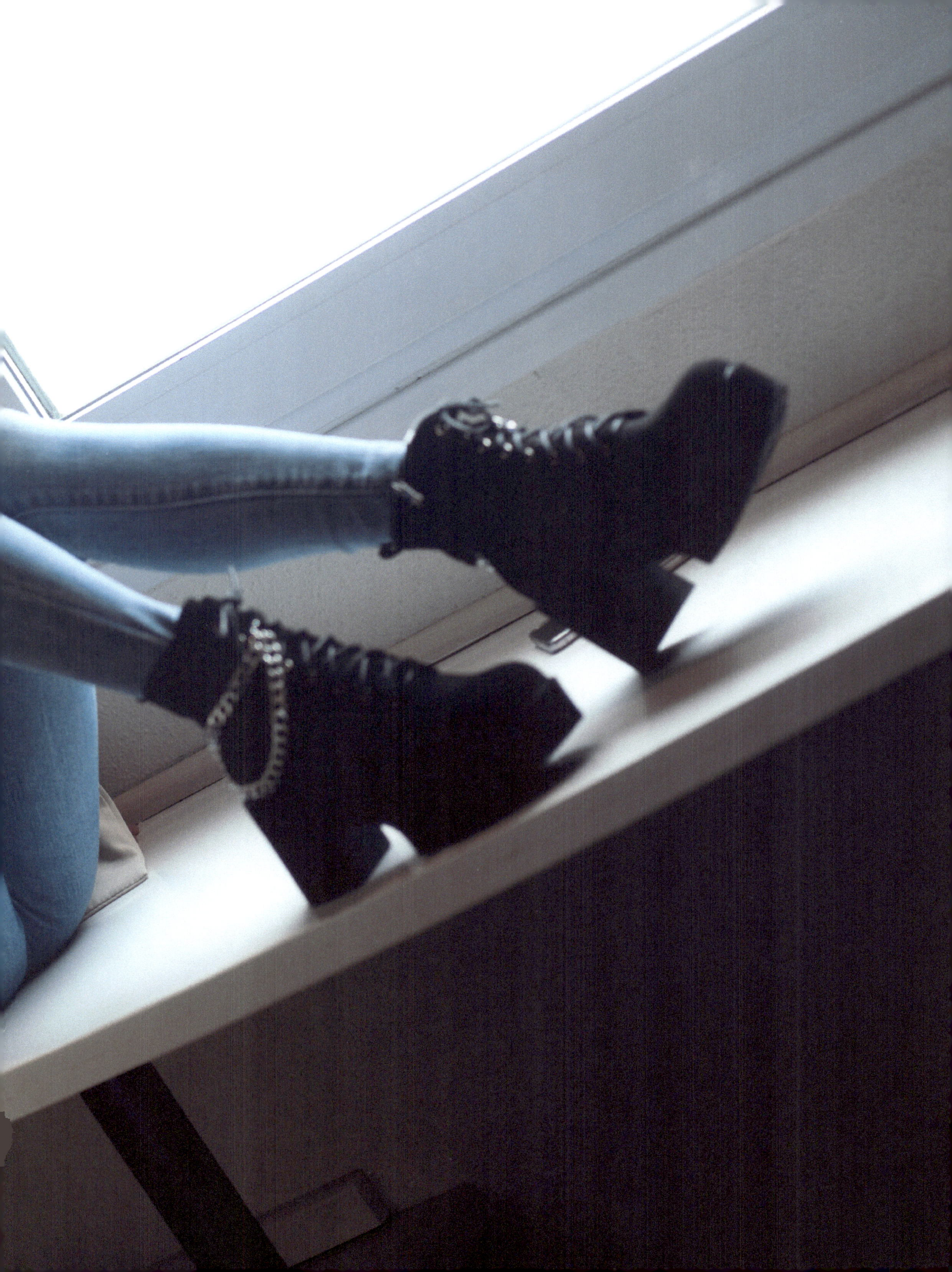

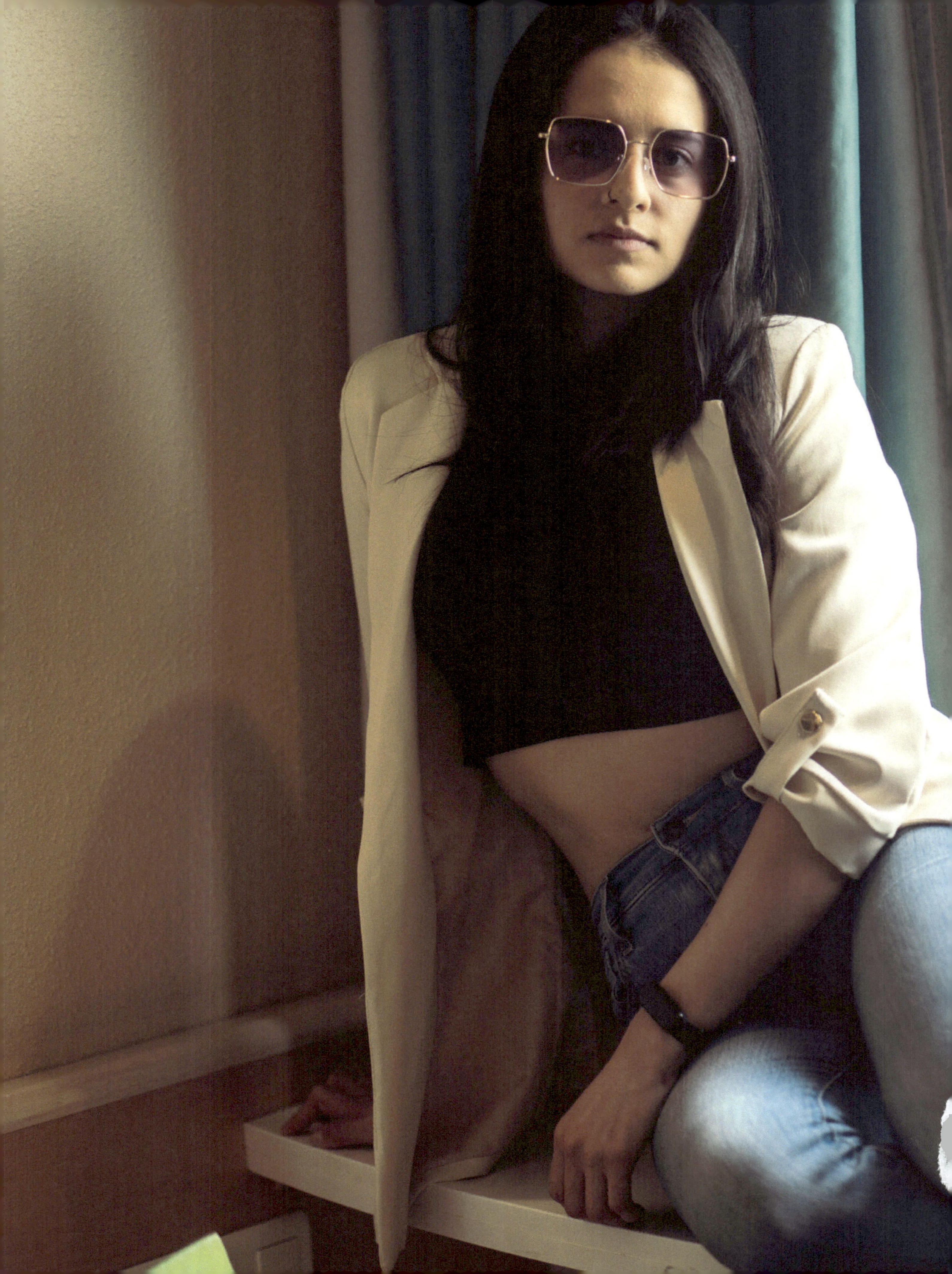

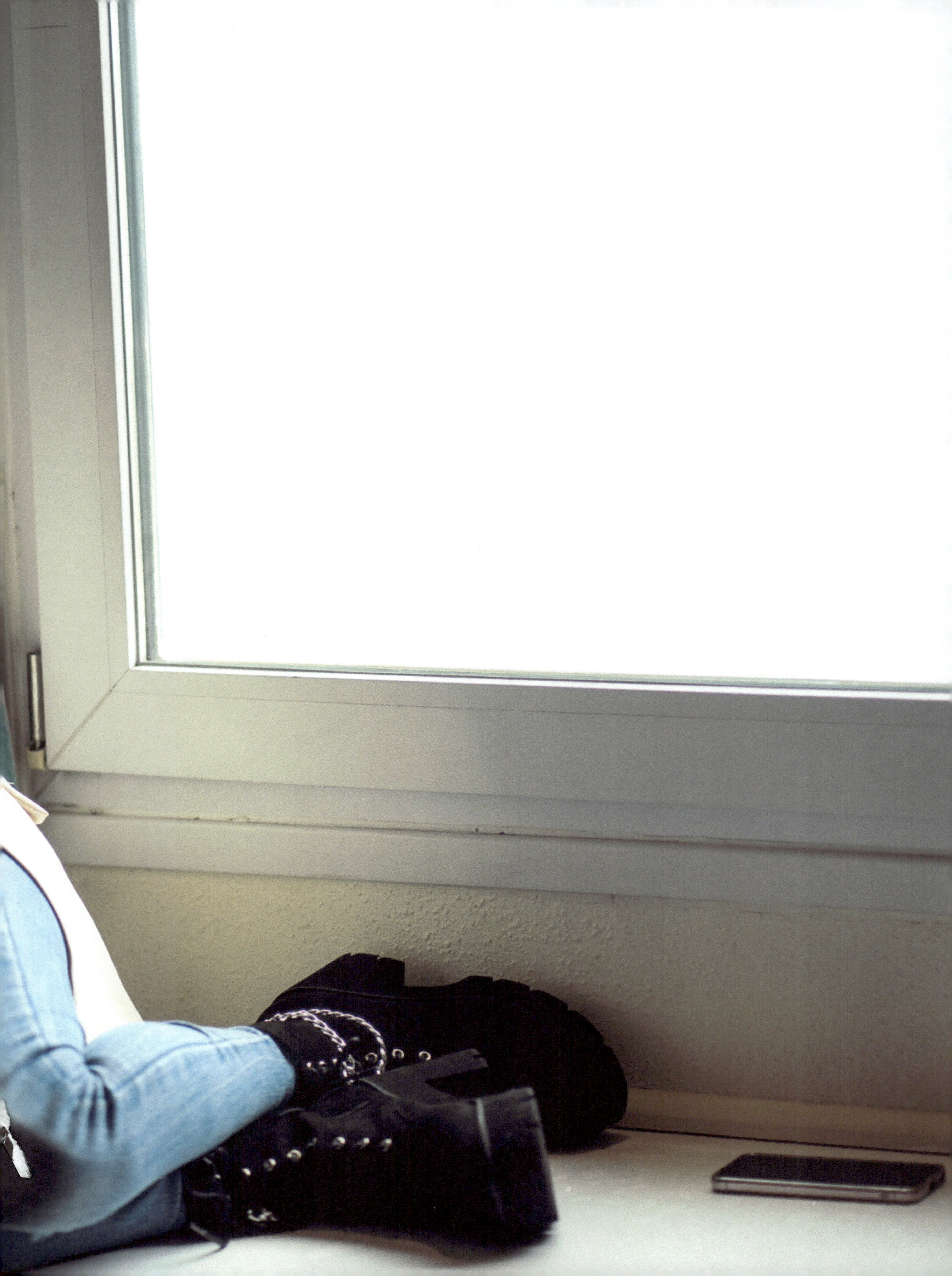

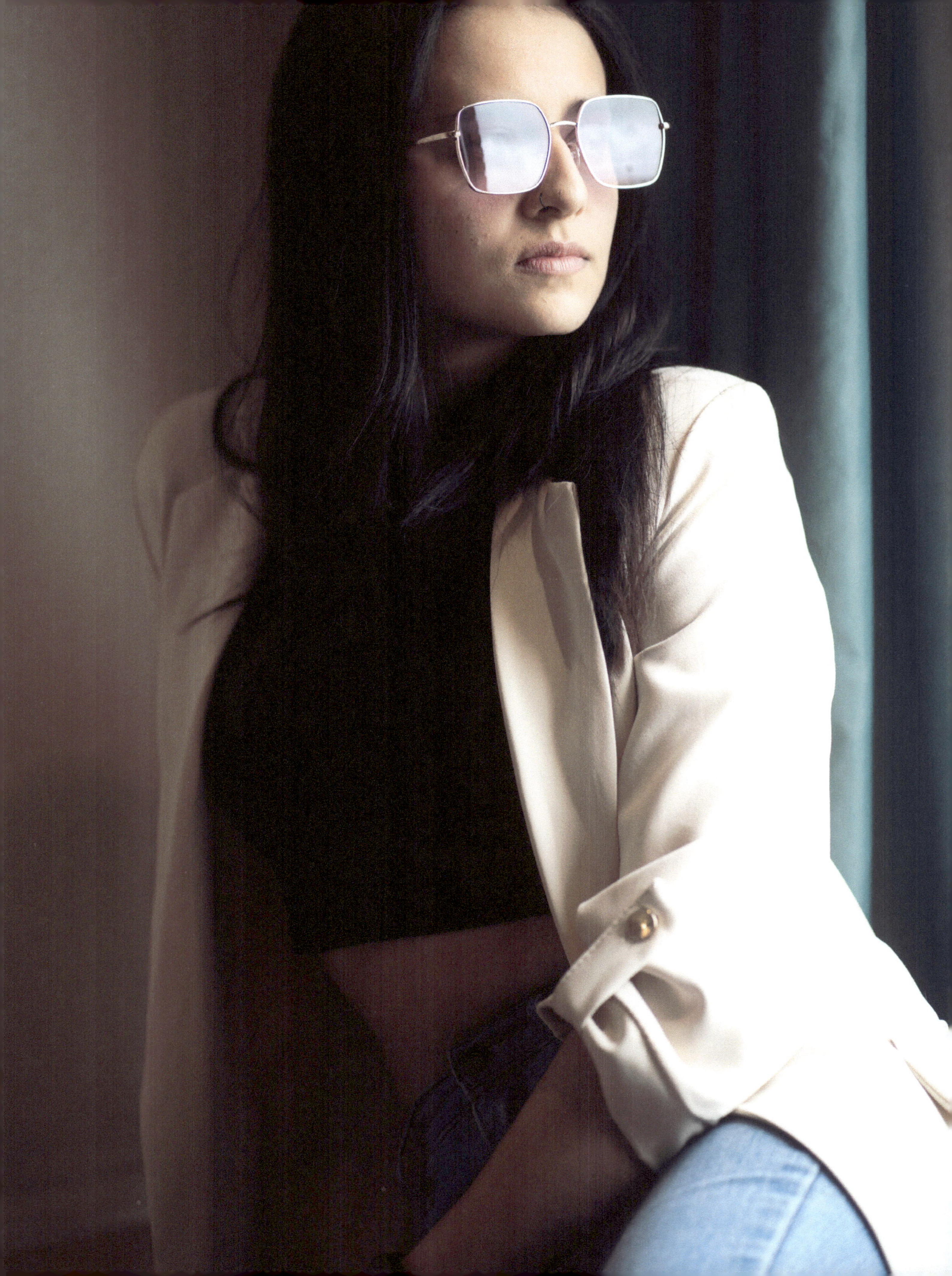

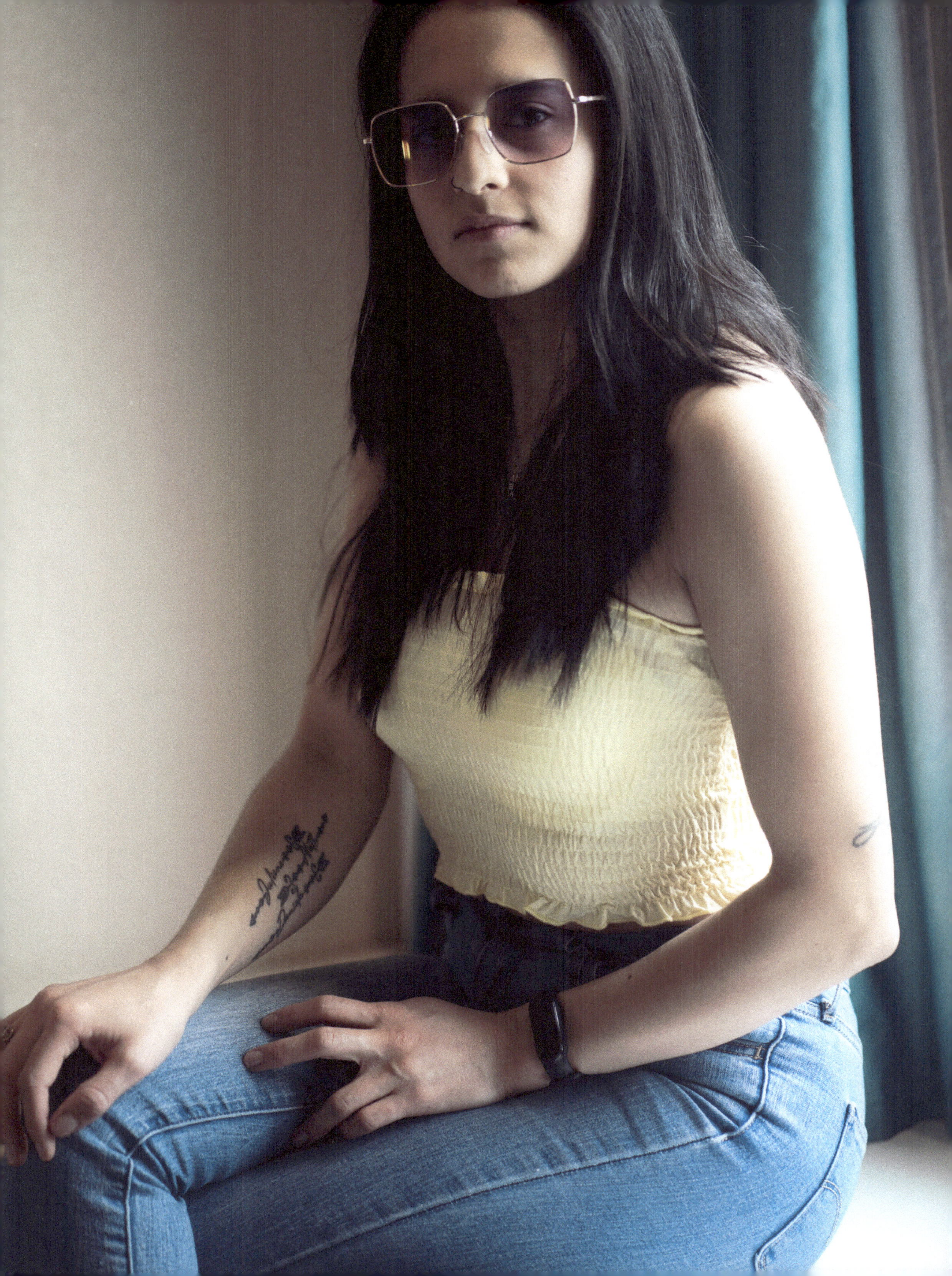

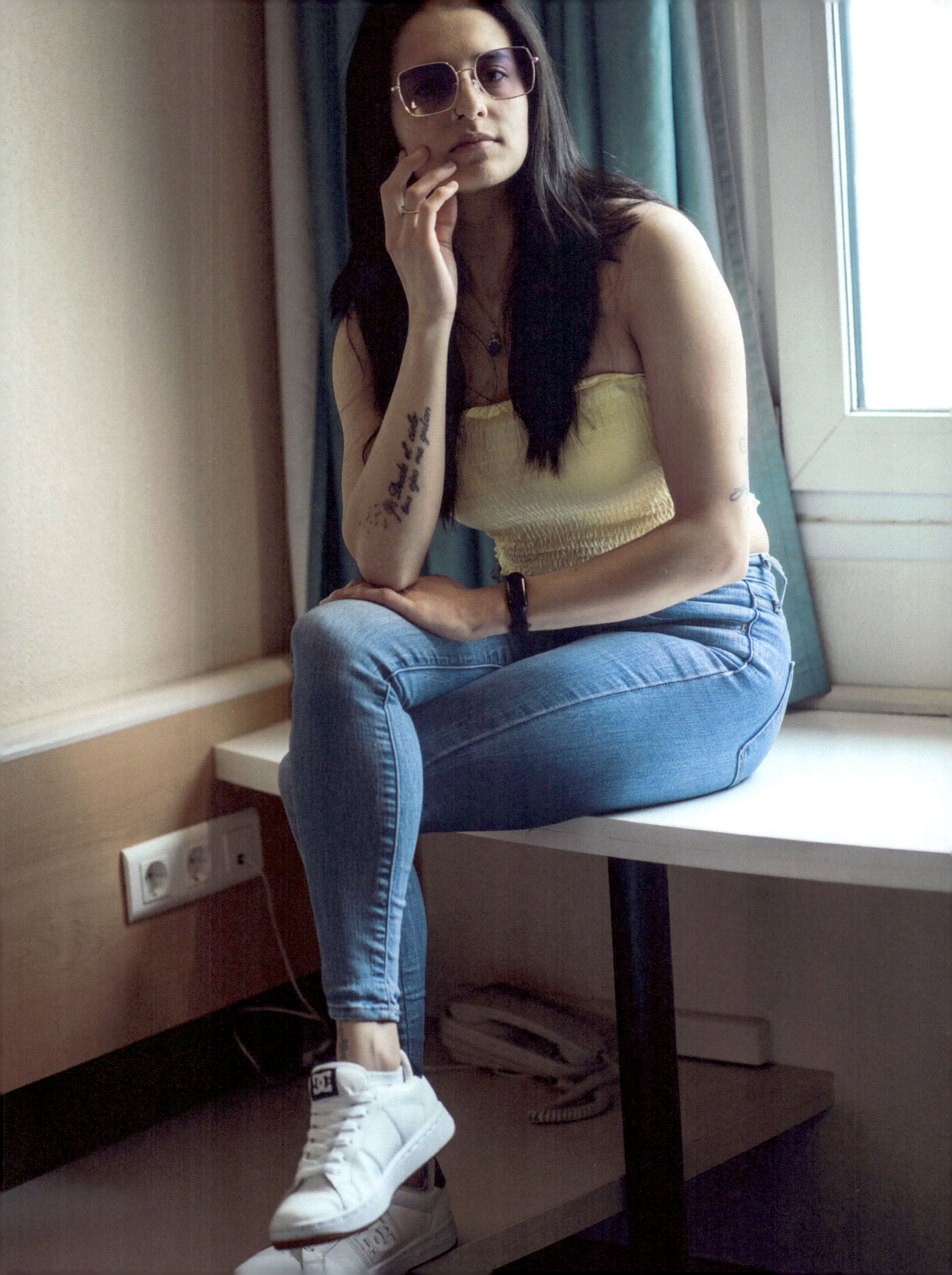

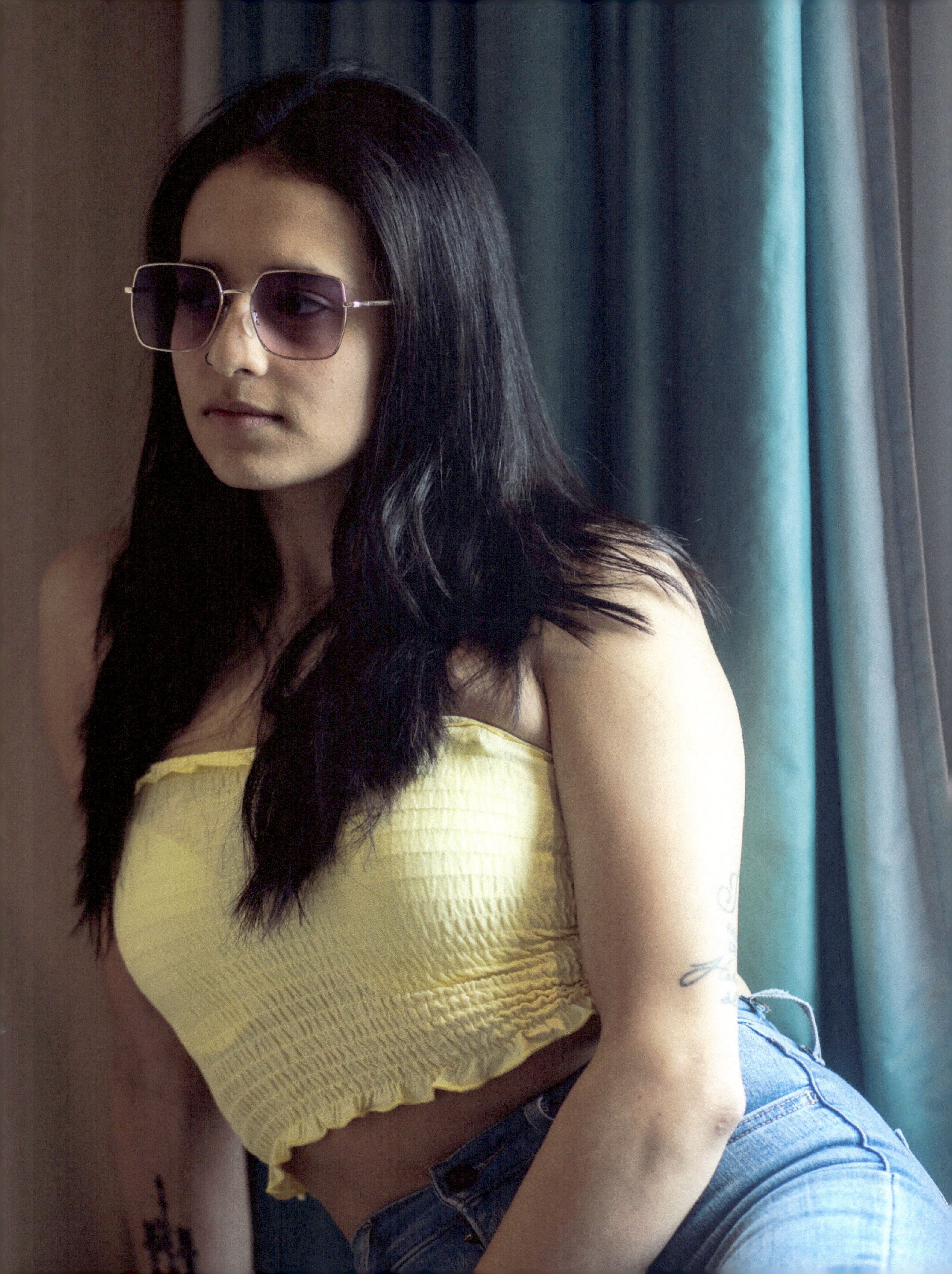

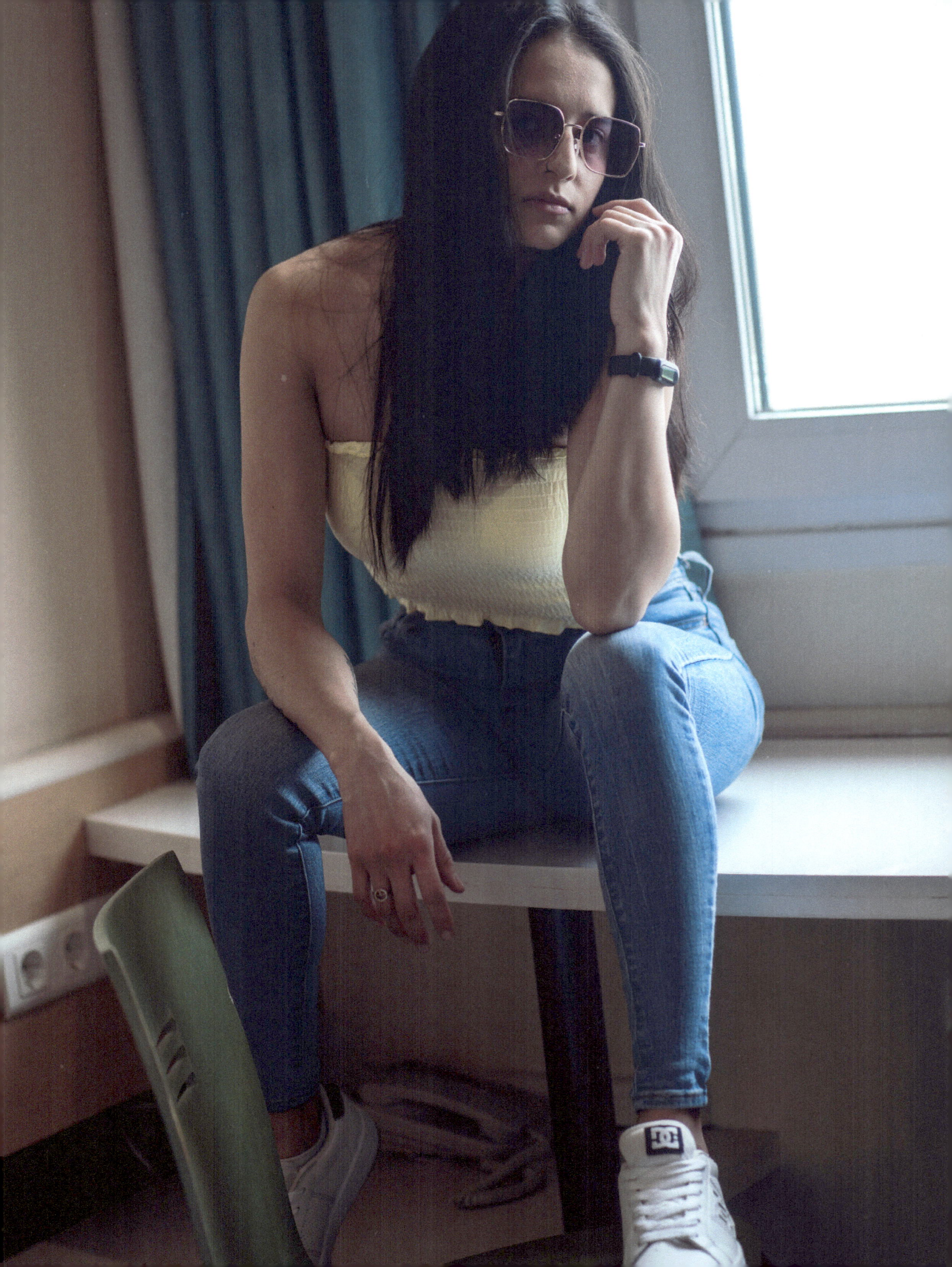

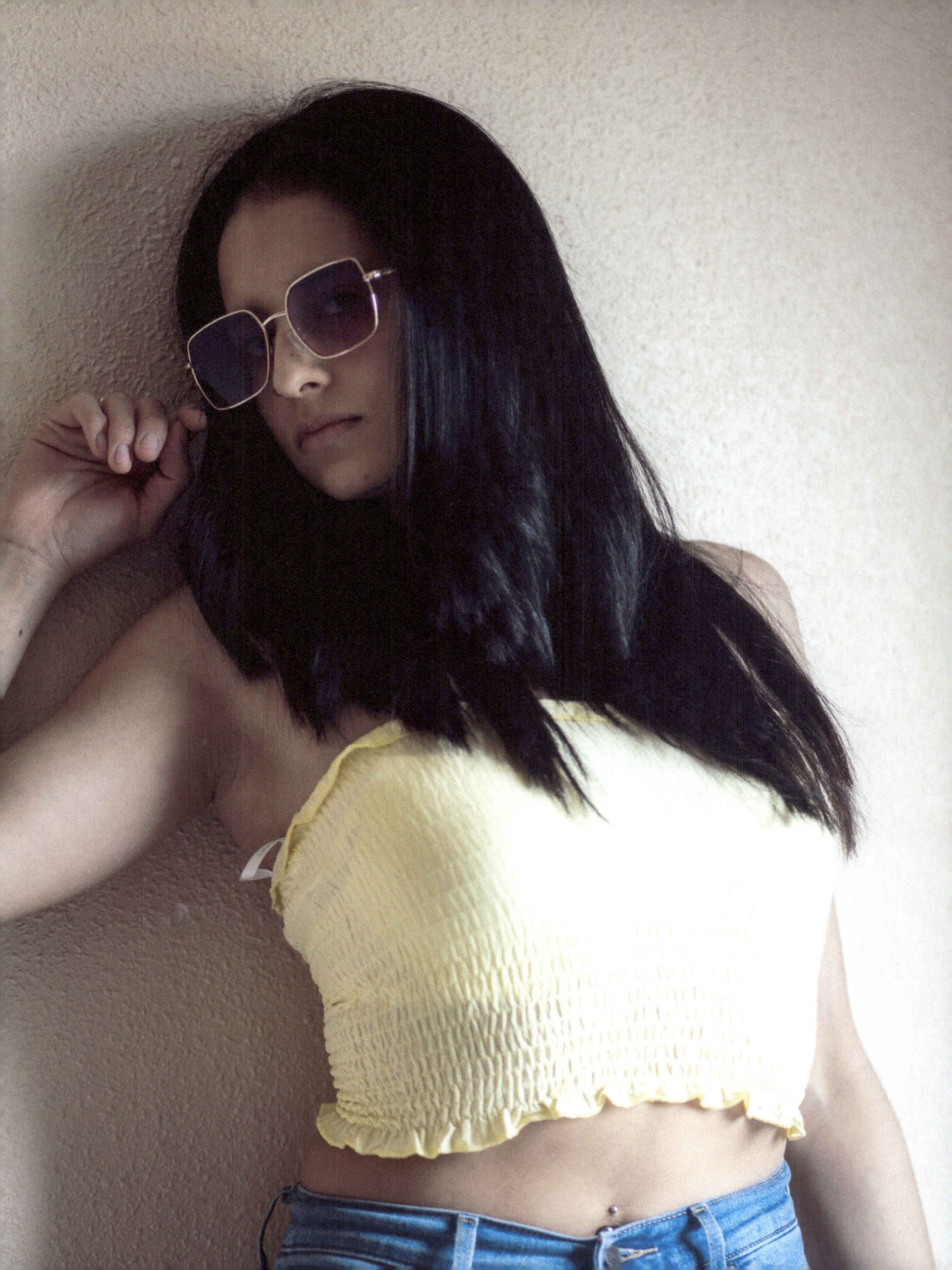

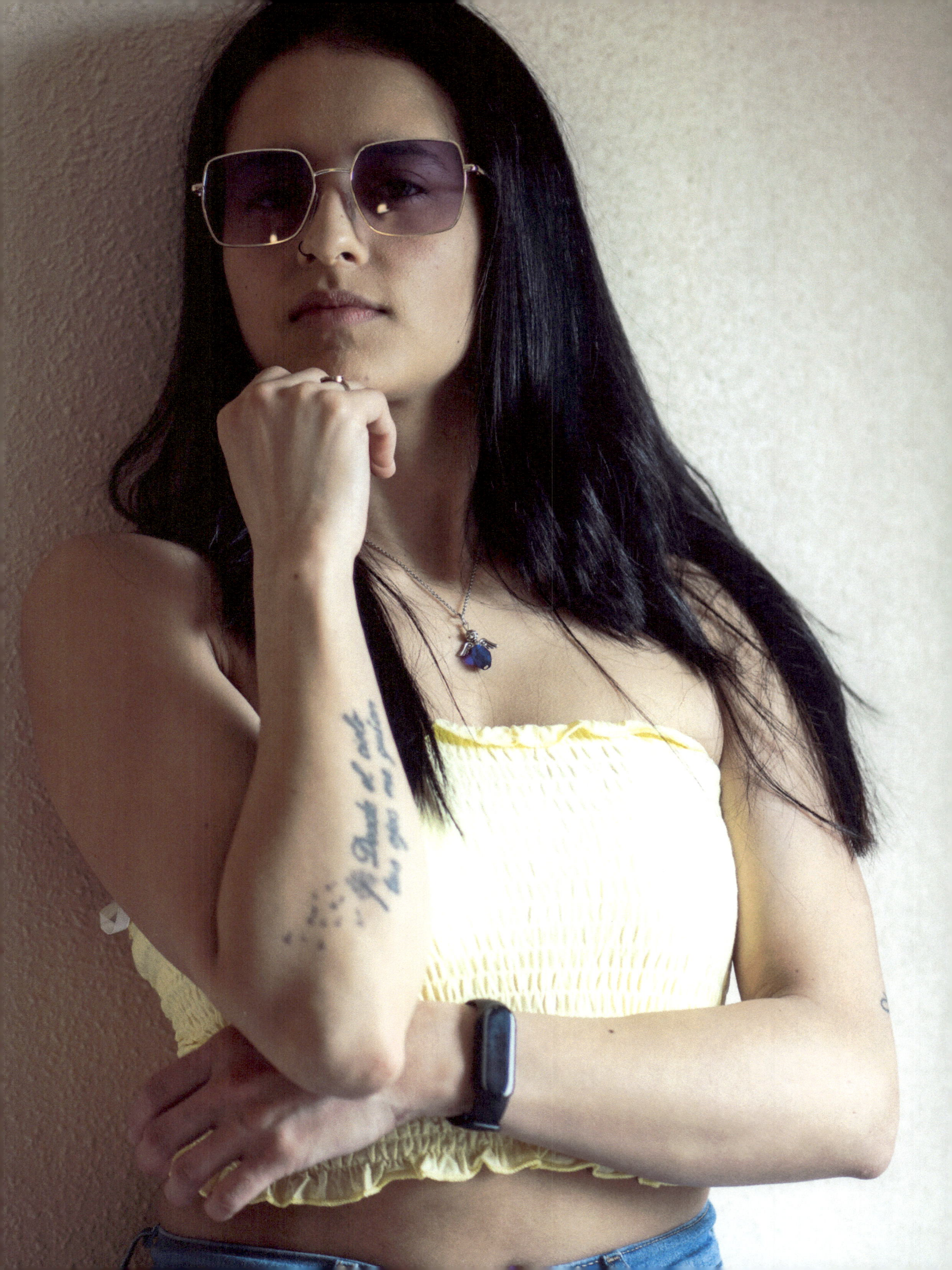

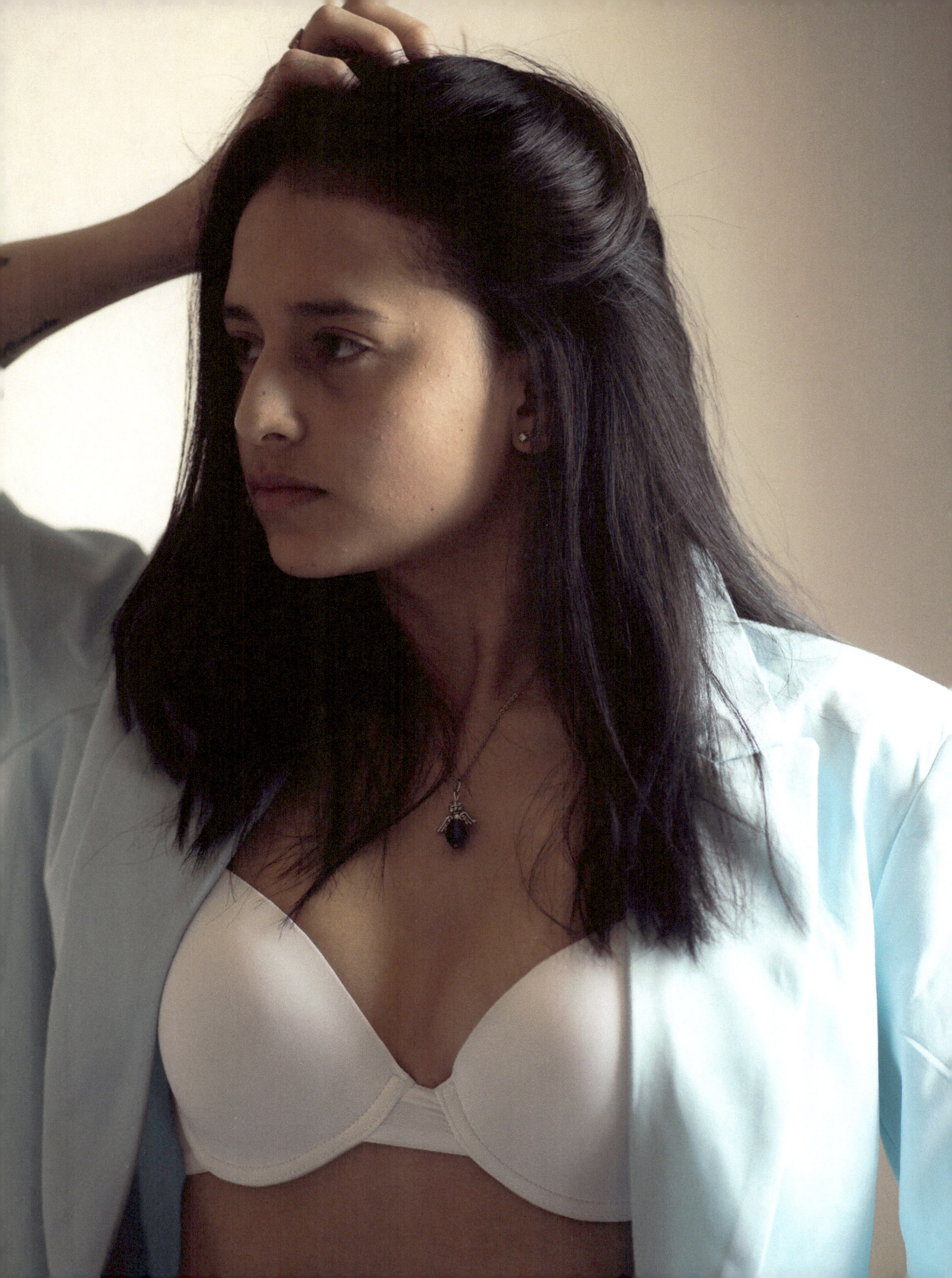

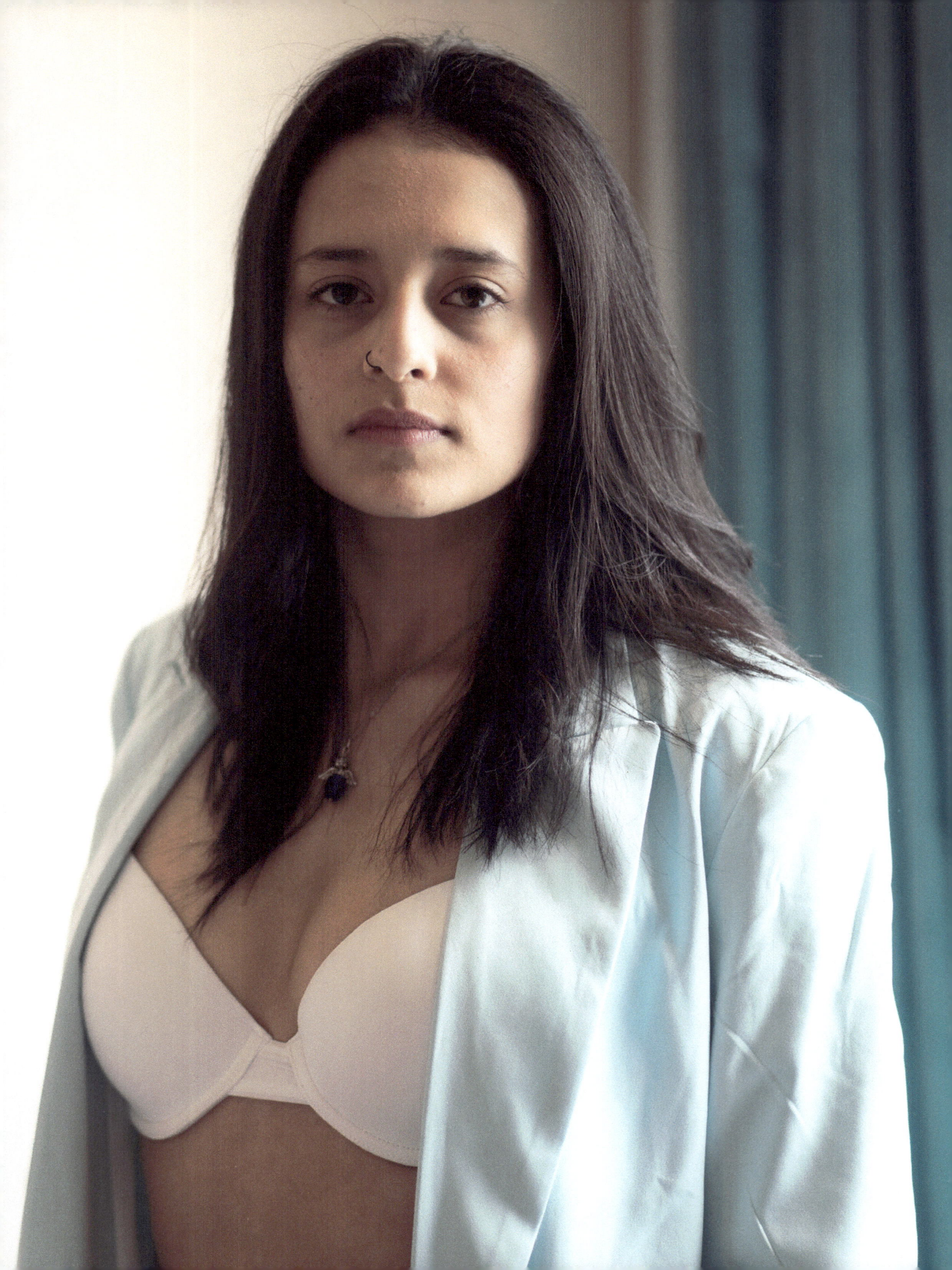

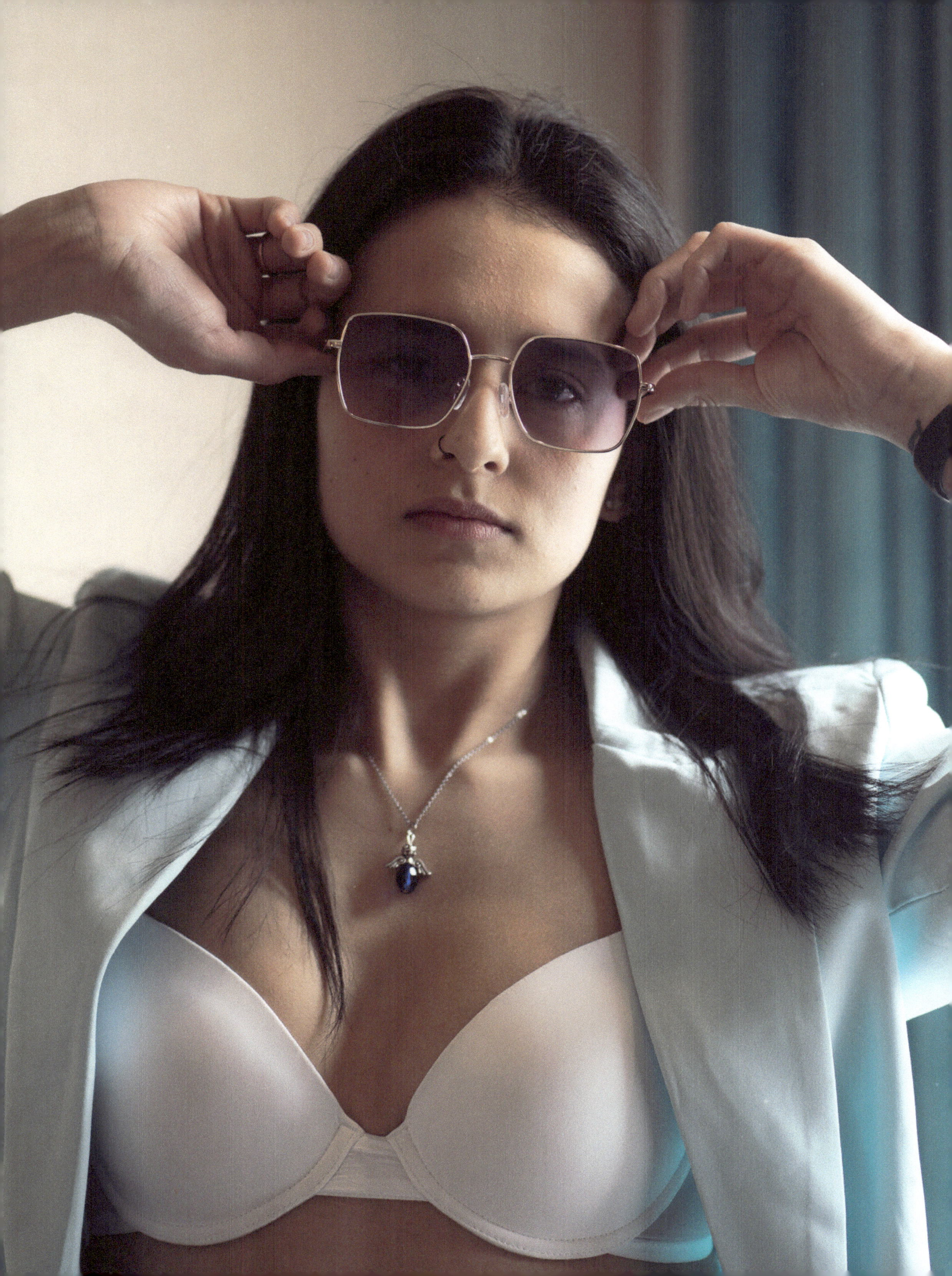

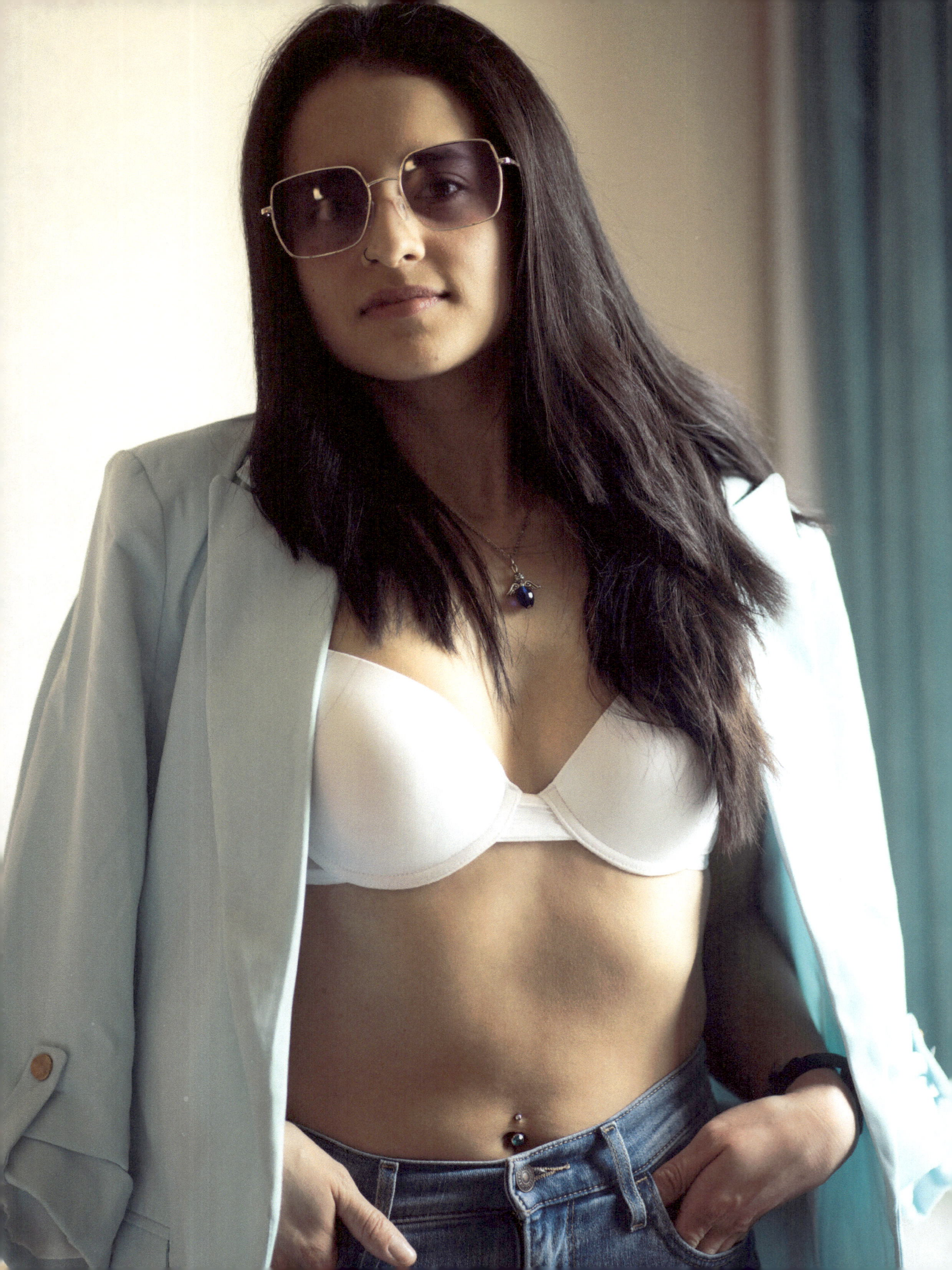

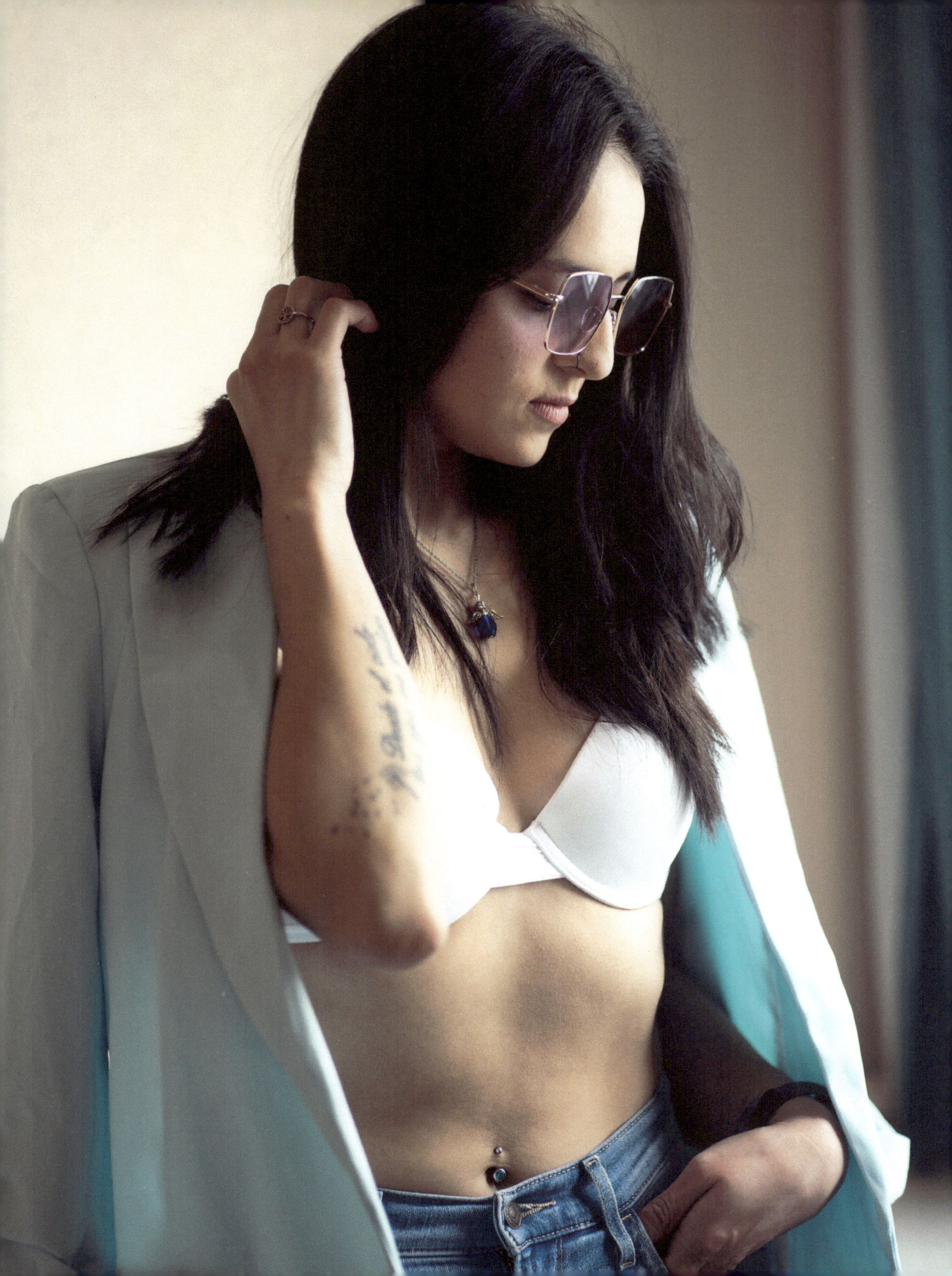

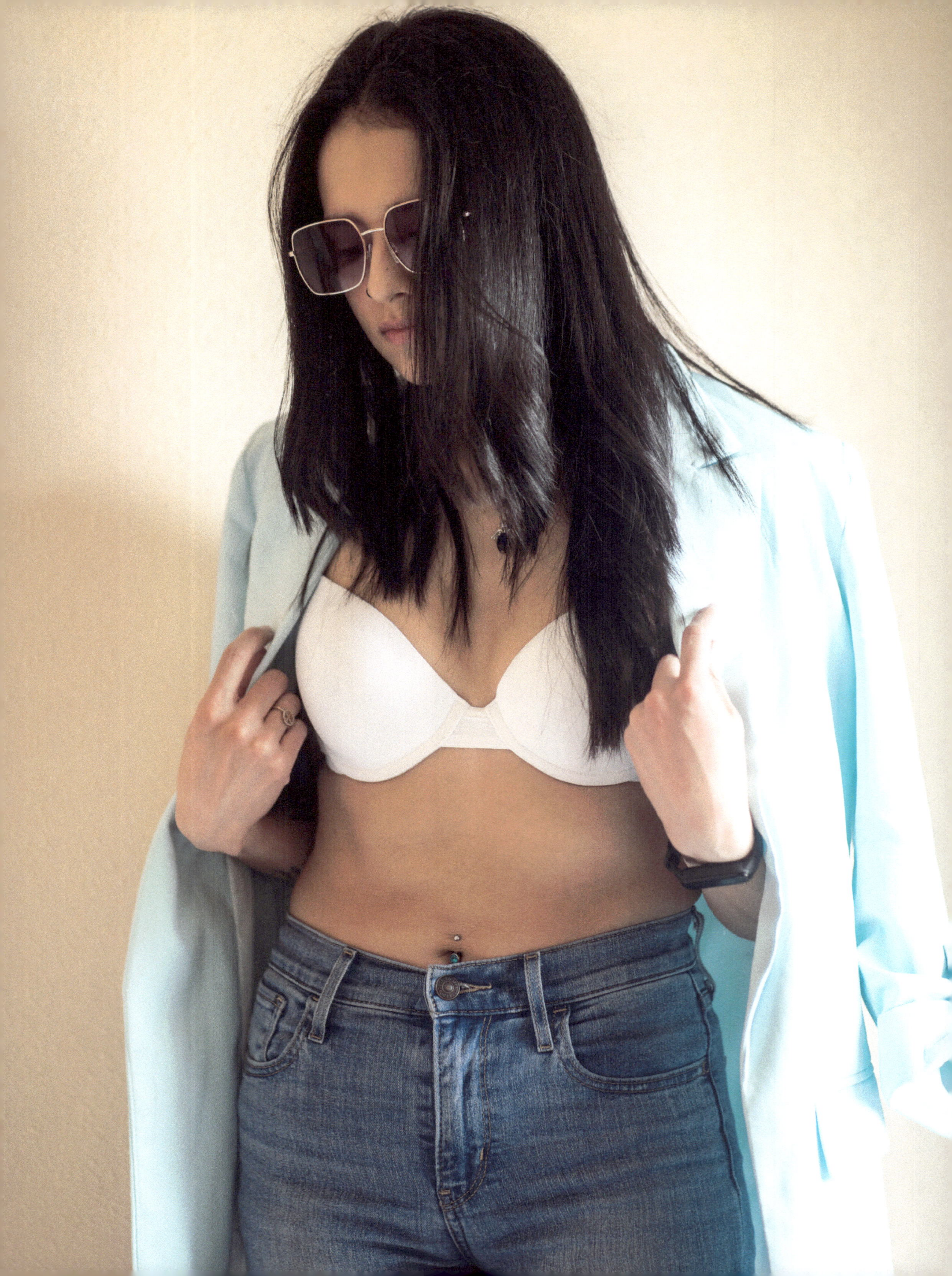

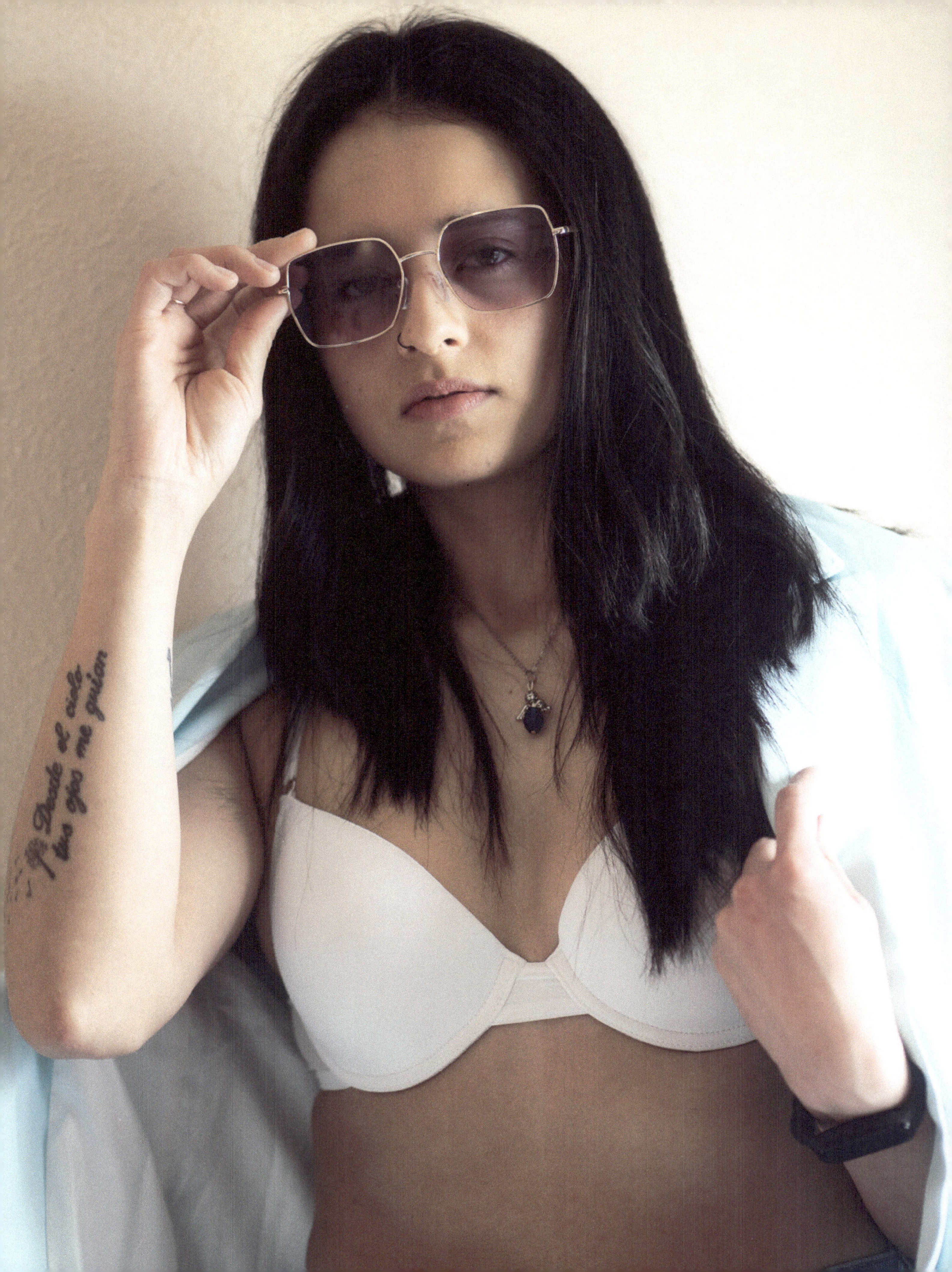
Desde el cielo
tus ojos me guian

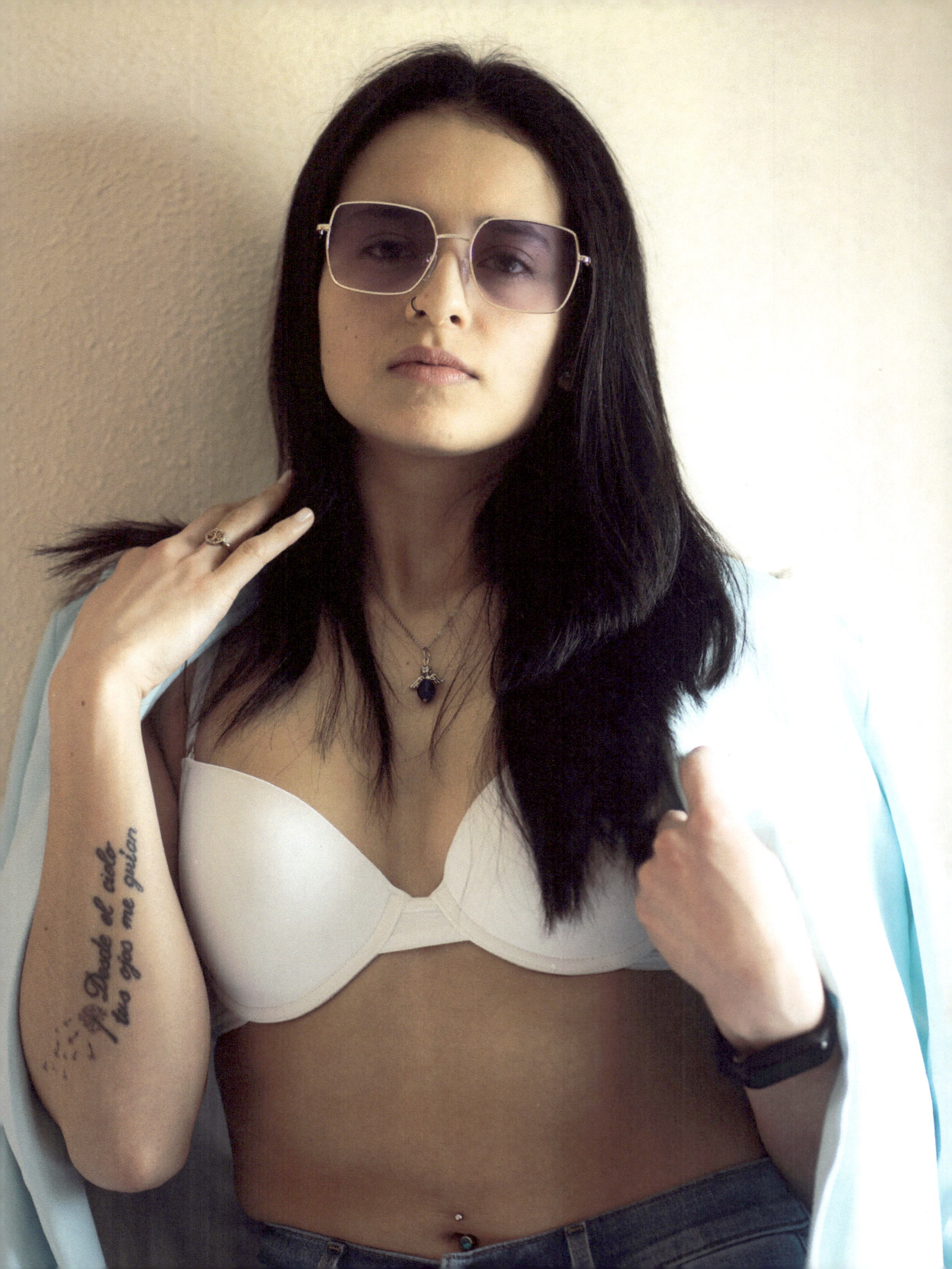
Desde el cielo
tus ojos me guian

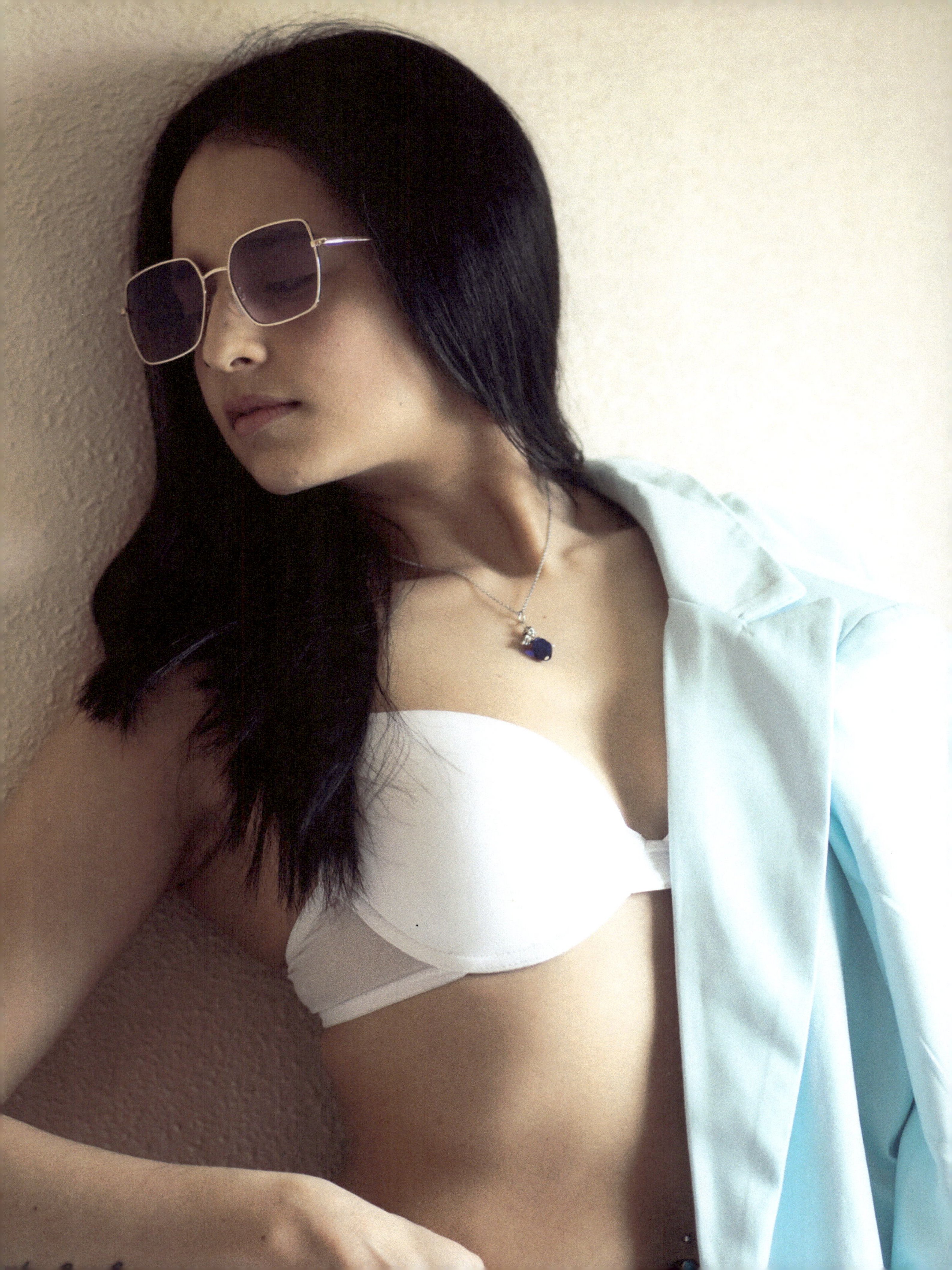

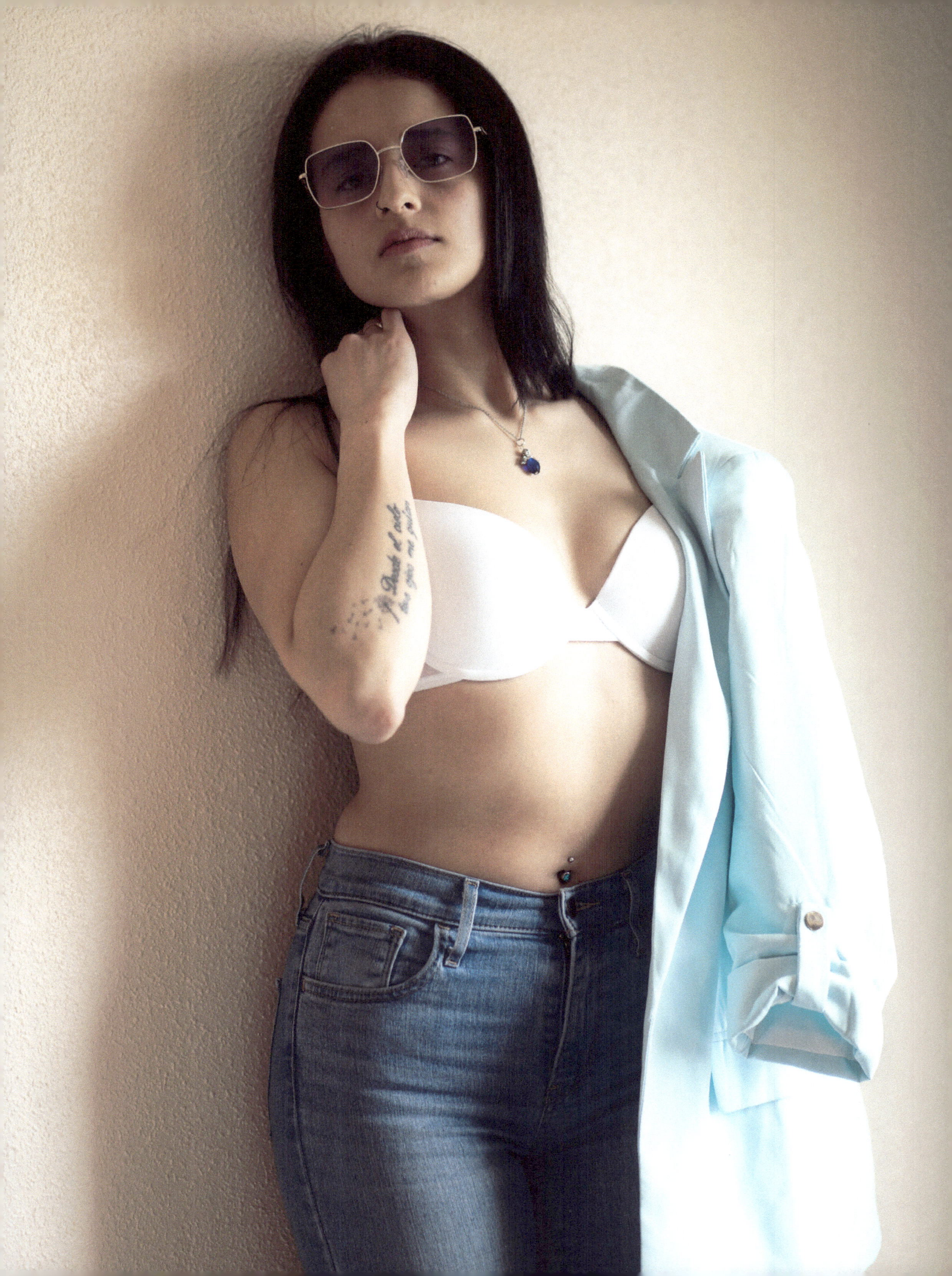

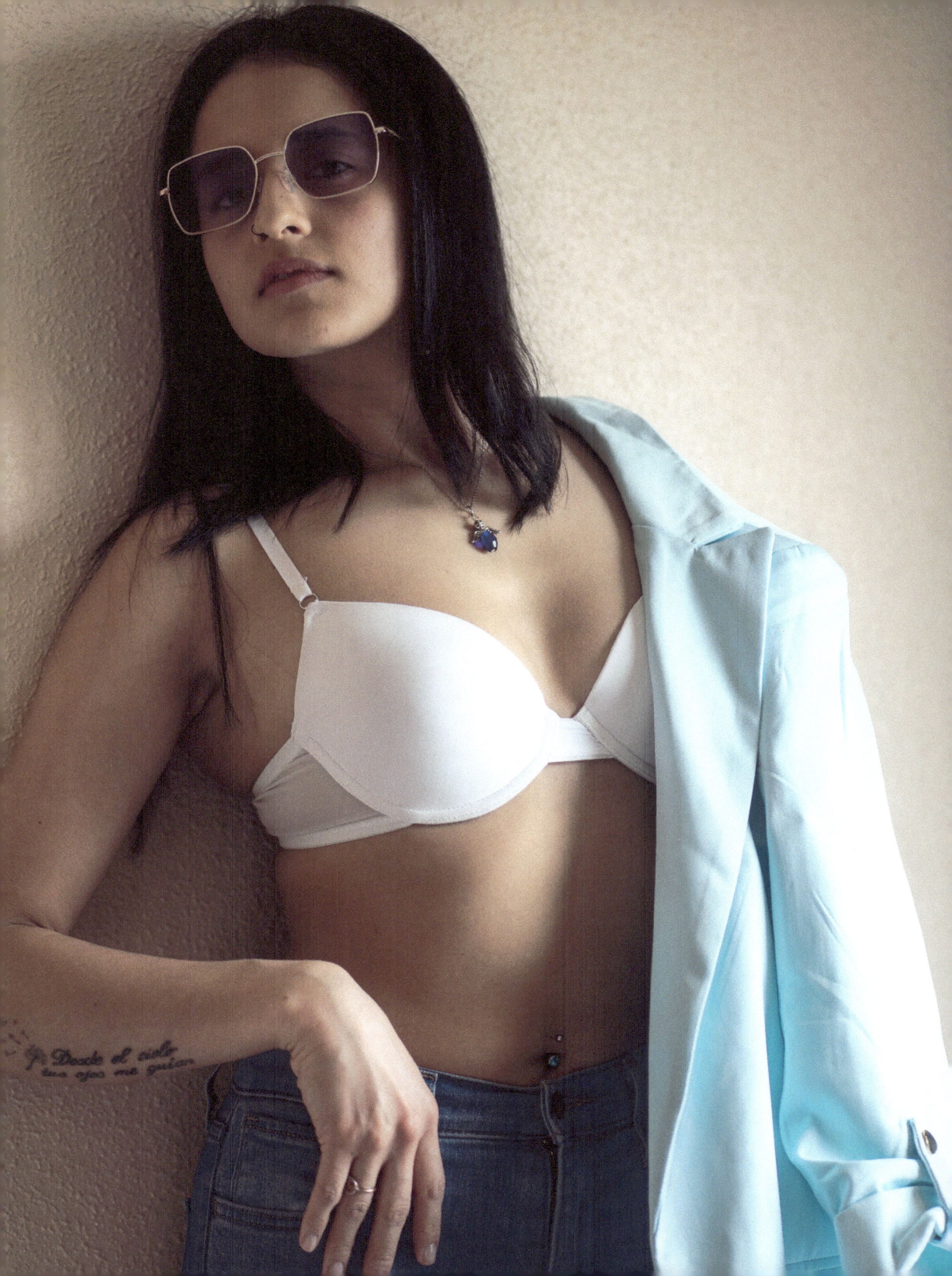

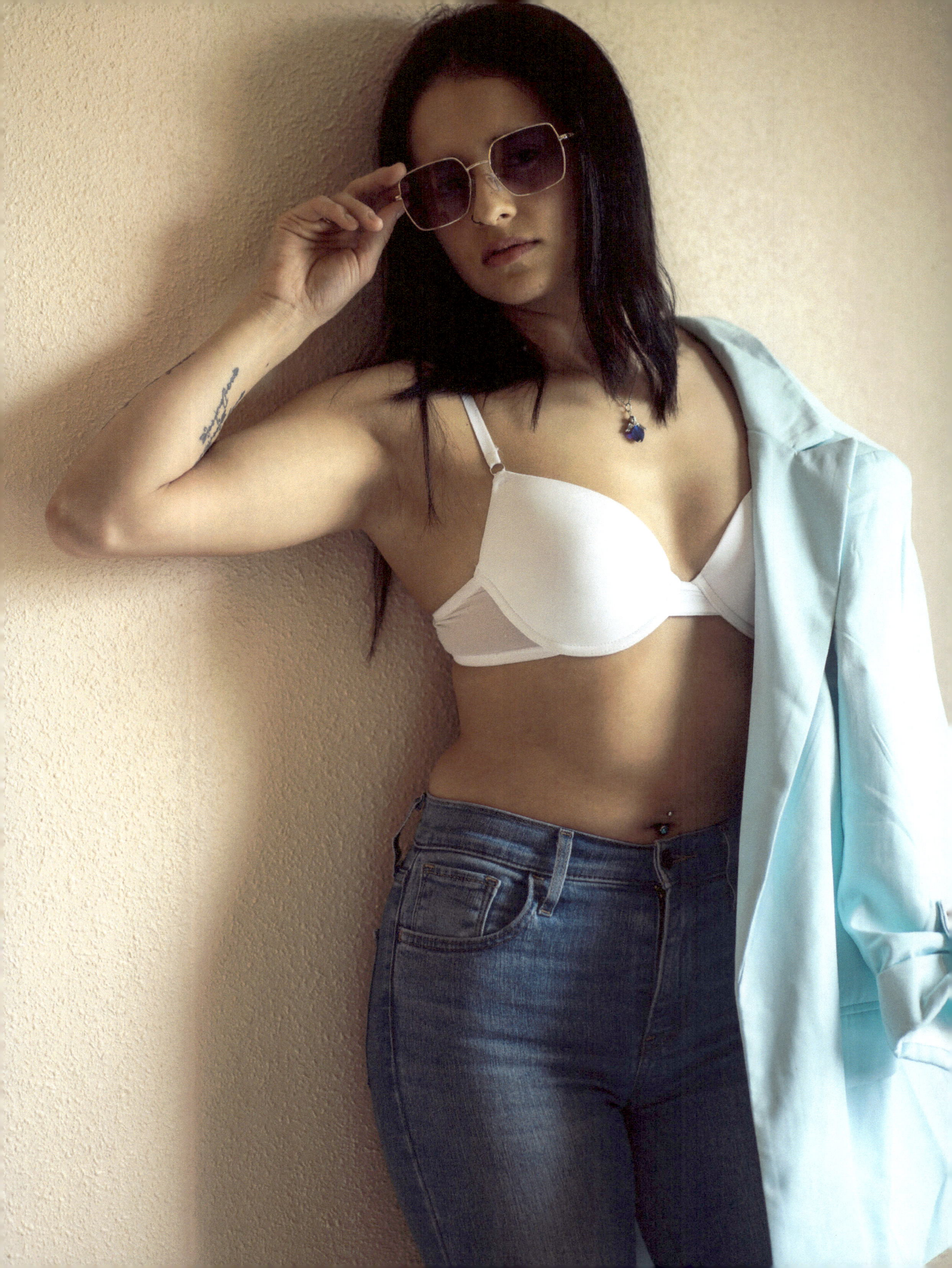

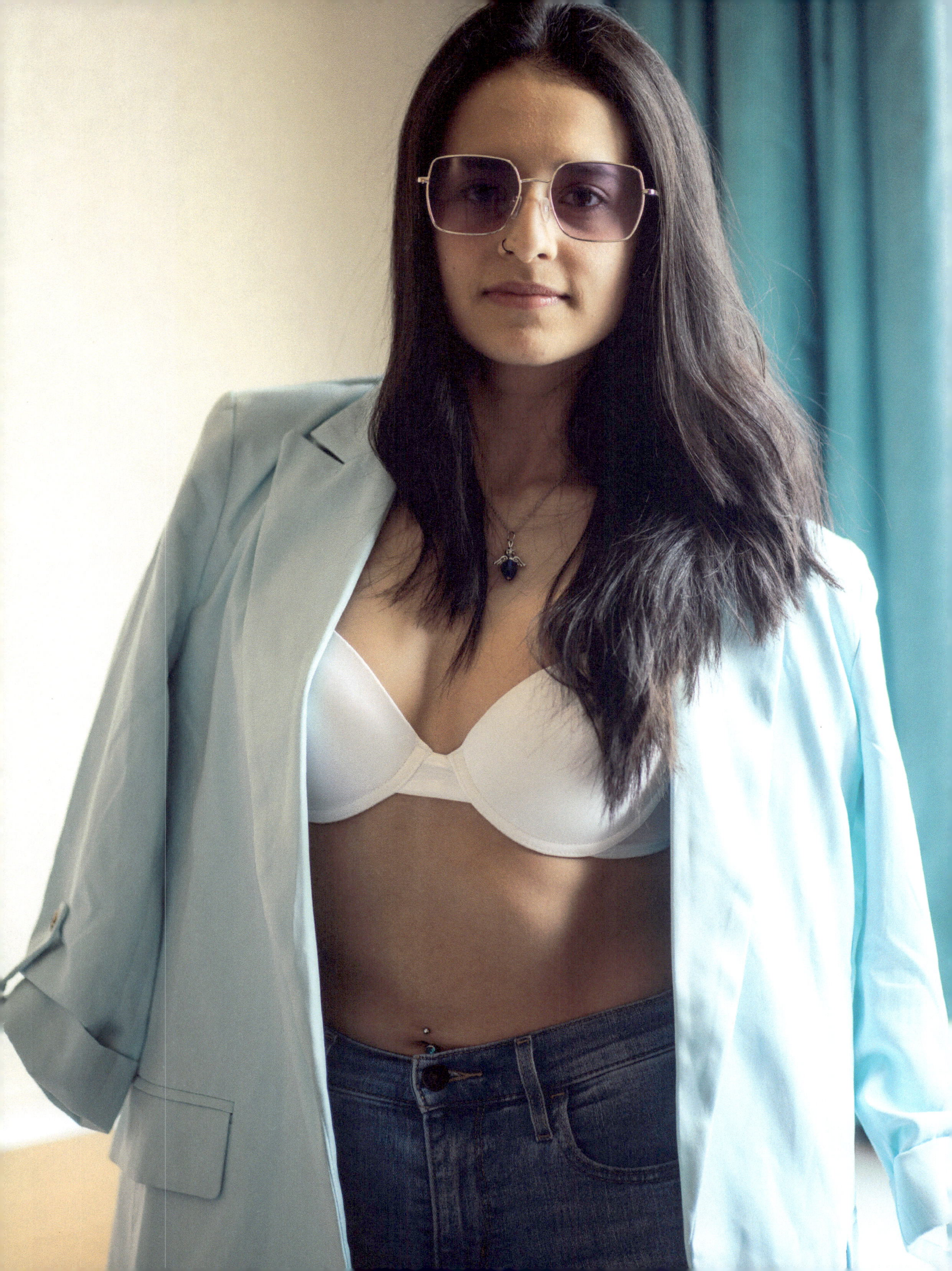

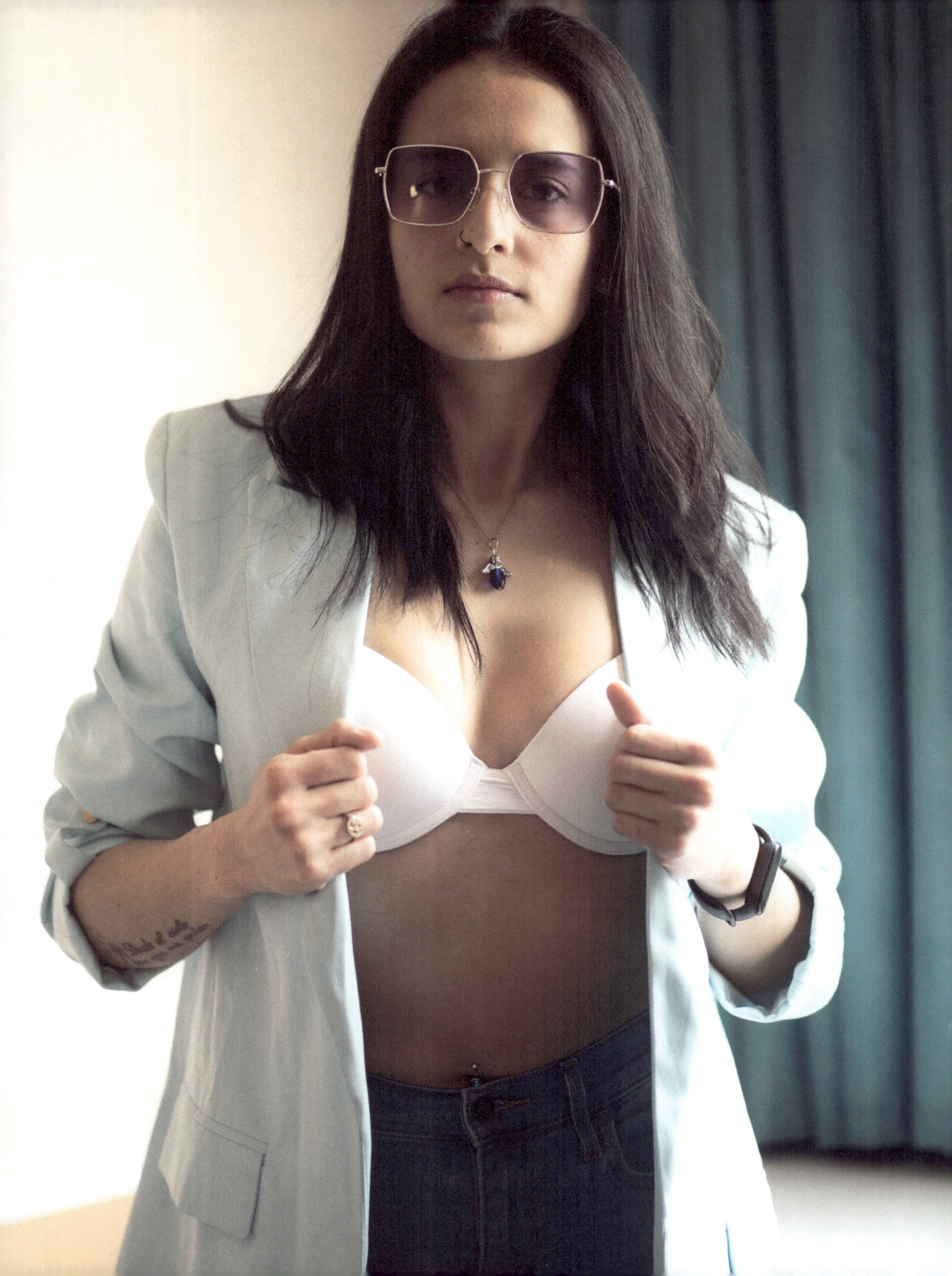

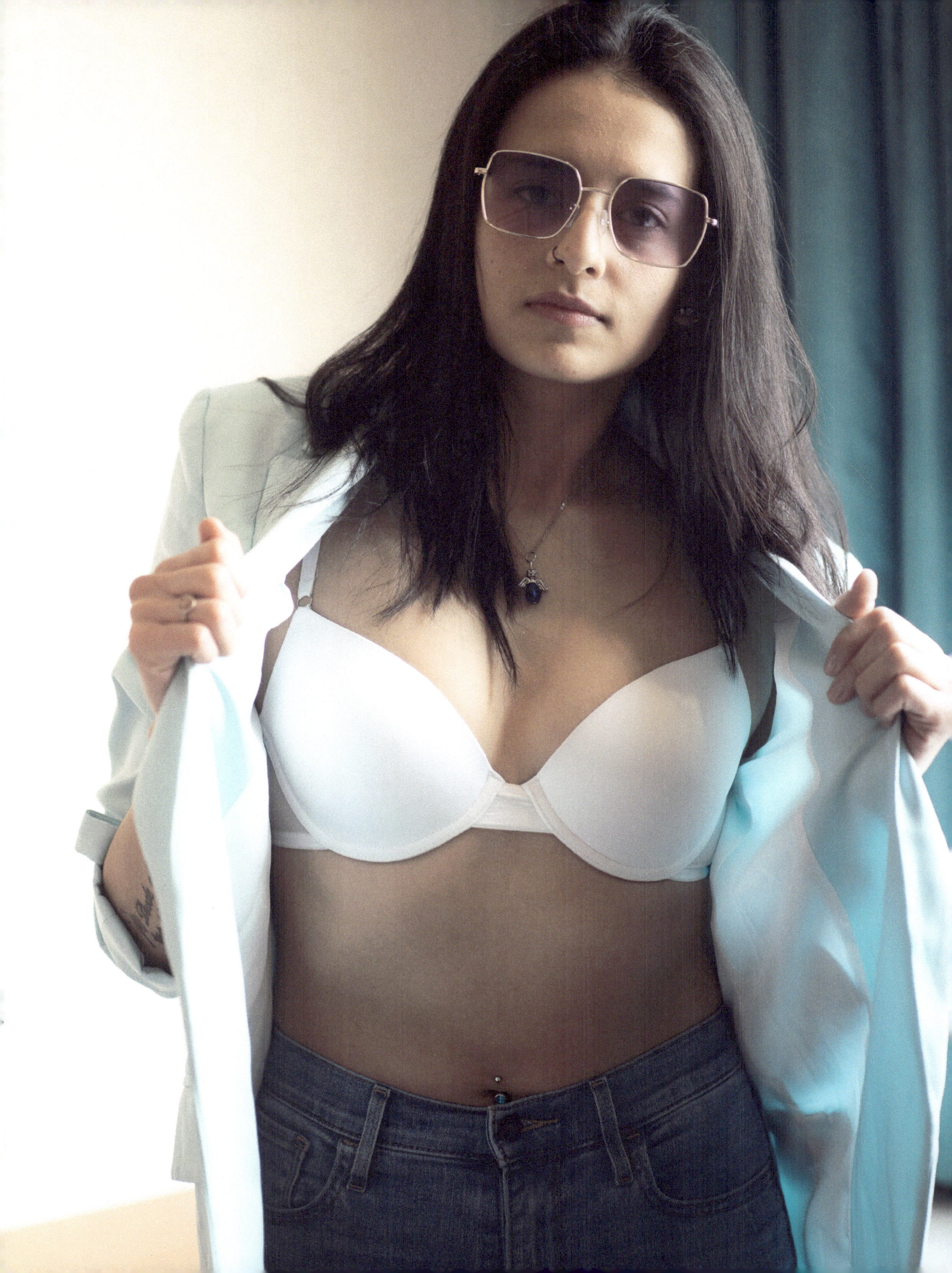

TOH

THE TRY ON HAUL MAGAZINE

By
Emporio Foto

www.ingramcontent.com/pod-product-compliance
Lightning Source LLC
Chambersburg PA
CBHW041521280526
45792CB00004B/1338
9798884392212